THE BIG STORY

The Big Story

Nick Page

LONDON • ATLANTA • HYDERABAD

13 12 11 10 09 08 07   7 6 5 4 3 2 1

First published 2007 by Authentic Media
9 Holdom Avenue, Bletchley, Milton Keynes, Bucks, MK1 1QR, UK

285 Lynnwood Avenue, Tyrone, GA 30290, USA

OM Authentic Media, Medchal Road, Jeedimetla Village,
Secunderabad 500 055, A.P., India

www.authenticmedia.co.uk

Authentic Media is a division of Send the Light Ltd., a company limited by guarantee
(registered charity no. 270162)

British Library Cataloguing in Publication Data

A catalogue record for this book is available from the British Library

ISBN 978-1-85078-726-6

Book Design by Nick Page

Cover Design by David Smart

Print Management by Adare Carwin

Printed and bound by J.H. Haynes & Co., Sparkford, Great Britain

CONTENTS

Time for a story.

Listen. I'm going to tell you the story. The Big Story. The Biggest Story of Them All.

This is the story of God and humans, the story of the world and all that's in it.

It's a Big Story made up of hundreds of little stories; a tapestry of miracles, a net full of shimmering fish.

It's a story about the beginning of time and the end of time and what happens in between. Stories don't come much bigger than that.

It has a lot to teach us, this story. But then all stories teach us something. Ugly ducklings can turn into swans. Giants can be chopped down to size. The bigger the story, the bigger the lessons to be learned.

So sit down, relax. Sit back and listen to the story.

And of course, all stories have to begin in a certain way.

Once upon a... hold on.

PROLOGUE

In which we see the invention of time, the creation of angels and witness a battle in heaven.

And that's *before* we really start.

PROLOGUE

CAST

God Creator of the universe, Supreme Being, etc.

Angels Beings created by God to do his will

Lucifer Head angel, rebel, fallen leader

0.1 The Beginning

Once before time there is a Great Big God...

And at some point, this Great Big God decides to make a universe.

He decides to make time itself.

He decides to make everything.

As a being who is present in all places and at all times simultaneously, it's obvious that I look like a very old bloke with a beard.

Once upon a time...

The traditional way to start a story. But not much good when you're dealing with God. Time means something different to him. He's outside it, wrapped around it, beyond the past, present and future tenses; a Being who is eternal, and who exists in the past, future and all points in between.

This is, perhaps the first thing to understand about God – or to *try* to understand at least: we're talking about a Being who is outside time, who *invented* time.

We are creatures of four dimensions – creatures of space and time.[1] But God is the Being of every dimension. And that's one of the most amazing themes of the Big Story; how this enormous God, this Being from completely outside our understanding and our physical existence, chooses to spend time with humans; more how he compresses himself, squeezes himself into our four-dimensional existence and becomes one of us.

But that is in the future.

A long way in the future.

1 Some scientists argue that there are at least ten dimensions. They may be right, they may be wrong, but one thing I do know: you wouldn't want to get stuck talking to them at parties.

0.2 The Angels

Before he creates the earth, God creates the angels.

The angels are to do his work. They are not like God, they cannot be everywhere at once, or all times at once. The angels are supposed to do what God wants, but he also gives them the ability to choose a different path. Which is exactly what happens.

One of them – some say the biggest and brightest and most beautiful of them all – rebels against God. He wants to take over. And he persuades others to join him.

There is a battle, but there can only be one victor. God throws the rebellious angels out of heaven. And their leader falls from those heights like a great, burning meteor, a ball of burning pain. He falls like a heavyweight boxer on the wrong end of a knockout punch. He falls like a falling star – which in a way, he is.

No-one knows where he lands, or into what screaming chaos he descends. But he is not destroyed in his fall. And he learns how to disguise himself.

Luke 10.18

Job 38.4–7

Only God knows when they were created, but it must have been before the creation of the world, because while God was flinging down fjords and rolling out rivers, the angels were singing and shouting for joy. A bit like having the radio on while you're working.

Angels are God's agents, his representatives, his avatars, the way he chooses to appear to people on earth.[1]

Crucially, angels were created to be free. That is, they have the ability to choose right from wrong. God sets people free in every possible way; even if they abuse that freedom by refusing him. And some angels did just that.

So they were cast out from heaven and became the evil, malevolent forces at work today.

Isa 14.12–20

Angels reappear throughout the Big Story. But it is important to remember their origin. They are created beings. Satan is powerful, but nowhere near as powerful as God. In the continual war between good and evil, Satan's opposite number is not God, but Michael, or Gabriel or some other angelic lieutenant with a name ending in '-el'.[2]

All right lads, 'Bohemian Rhapsody', key of C...

1 And you can forget all the wings and the cute chubby cherubs. When humans meet angels in the Bible the normal response is abject fear and a quick change of trousers.

2 Not 'Spaniel'.

ACT 1
THE FATHERS

In which we watch the creation of the world, meet the first humans, see evil infect the world, get wet in the great flood; meet Abraham and his family and finally end up in Egypt.

ACT 1: THE FATHERS

1.1	Creation
1.2	Adam and Eve
1.3	The Fall
1.4	Noah and the Flood
1.5	Babel and Abraham
1.6	The Great Promise
1.7	Three Visitors
1.8	The Test of Abraham
1.9	Jacob and Esau
1.10	Jacob Wrestles God
1.11	Joseph

CAST

Adam	First man
Eve	First woman
Serpent	Lucifer in a snakeskin outfit
Noah	Ark builder
Abraham	Father of the Israelite nation
Sarah	His wife
Hagar	Their slave girl
Ishmael	Son of Abraham and Hagar
Isaac	Son of Abraham and Sarah
Rebekah	Isaac's wife
Esau	Eldest son of Isaac and Rebekah
Jacob	Twin brother of Esau, youngest son of Isaac and Rebekah, but only by a minute
Joseph	Eleventh son of Jacob

Also various builders, angels and eleven other sons of Jacob, etc.

1.1 Creation

At first there is just a great big, black, blank nothing. It has no form, this nothingness; no shape. It is just a deep, dark absence.

So God calls for light and that is day one.

On the second day, God drives the liquid darkness back by shaping the sky around the world.

On the third day he makes land, and gathers the waters into the seas. Then he covers the land with trees and plants; seed, shoot, fruit and flower; clothing the land to keep it warm.

On the fourth day, he scatters stars in the sky and sets the sun and moon to work, bringing time and seasons to life.

On the fifth day, he fills the sea with fish and the air with birds and he tells them to get breeding.

On the sixth day, he makes the land bring forth animals; wild and tame, fierce and furtive, large and small.

But something is missing; the cherry on the cake, the salt in the soup.

Gen 1.2–25

Right at the beginning, from his first words in the Bible, God is a light-bringer, one who illuminates the darkness

But the light does more than that. The light drives the waters back. Water features a lot in the creation account. Here it is an image of dark, purposeless chaos. God is the Creator, bringing form out of formlessness, shape and purpose out of the ever-shifting, ever uncertain deep.

Job 6.18, 26.7; Is 24.10; 1 Sam 12.21

The Hebrew words used to describe this first scene – a formless void – are used elsewhere to describe emptiness, wastelands and even the futility of worshipping false gods.[1]

The desire to create is the desire to give something form and substance and meaning. Every act of creation echoes that first act of God on the first day; a pushing back of chaos, a bringing of light, the beginning of shape and meaning. Every time we tell a story, we are doing what God did – speaking things into order, giving events substance and meaning.

Gen 1.2; Job 33.4; Ps 104.30; Jn 1.1

God does this with Word and Spirit. The Word is spoken, the Spirit hovers over the waters; God in his three parts – the Father, Son and Holy Spirit – creating, nurturing, separating order from chaos.[2]

The stage is prepared. Now the Big Story can really get going.

---

1 The Hebrew words are *tōhû* (without form) and *bōhû* (void). How many people live *tōhû-bōhû* lives?

2 John's phrase 'In the beginning was the Word...' identifies Jesus as the Word, the creative power behind creation.

Jn 1.1

1.2 Adam and Eve

After the animals, God decides to make man.

God: We'll make man in our own image, just like us, and let's give him the earth to look after – all the animals and fish and plants and birds.

Some say he makes man first, from the dust of the ground. But the man is lonely, and in this good world, this loneliness is the one jarring note.

So God puts the man to sleep and takes one of his ribs, and from that he creates woman.

The man is called Adam, the woman is Eve. God puts the man and the woman in a garden he has made for them. They are to live there and look after it.

And all this is perfect. The world is as good as it could be; the kind of good you can only get when nothing is dirty and old and everything is shiny and new and really well-made. It is untouched by fear or unhappiness or greed or pain or any of those things which are to come later.

That's how good it is.

And after all this – on the seventh day – God rests.

Sure the leaves work OK now, but what happens in autumn?

At every stage of God's creative task, he checks it for quality control. Everything in it is good. Even the humans. (Ah yes, the humans. We'll come back to them in a moment.)

Can God ever sleep? Does he need to? Doubtful. If God turned off for a moment then surely the universe would collapse, like a bouncy castle when you turn the air pump off. But, anyway, here, he rests. He spends the seventh day resting and thinking and maybe enjoying all that he has made.

Gen 2.1–3

And by doing so he sends out a message to humans – that life is not all about work; it's also about reflection and rest and renewal. He's God – he doesn't need to rest, but he knows that we do.[1] He wants us to do the right thing, so he gives us a demonstration. And this idea of resting once a week they were later to call the Sabbath.

Gen 1.26–27

That's where they got the idea from: God's day off.

Gen 1.26–31, 2.15–25

As for man and woman, there are different accounts in Genesis (or the same account, depending on your point of view). But whatever the case, humans are special, there is something different about them. Notice the care God takes of it all. He doesn't just leave humanity to get on with it. He gives them life, but more than that, he gives them a place to live and a way of living.

1 After all, if he really does need to rest then we should move our church services. It's pointless having a church service on God's day off.

1.3 The Fall

In the garden, there is only one rule. In the garden are two special trees: the tree of the knowledge of good and evil, and the tree of life. God tells Adam and Eve not to eat of the tree of the knowledge of good and evil.

So all is well. Until, one day, sly and slippery, the serpent slithers out of the foliage. (He isn't a serpent at all, he is the leader of those fallen angels, Lucifer the Light-bringer, who has slipped into something less comfortable.)

Serpent: See that fruit? Very tasty, that fruit.

Eve: We're not allowed to taste it.

Serpent: *(slyly)* Did God really say that? Or is he just keeping the good stuff for himself?

So Eve is swayed. She eats the fruit and it tastes so good, she takes some to Adam.

Eve: Eat this. It's really good.

Adam: *(shocked)* What have you done?

Adam takes the fruit and has a bite. And suddenly, they see things with new eyes. The colours are dimmer, the light less bright. And clothes – they never worried about clothes before, but now they feel... ashamed.

So they hide in the foliage. Like the snake did.

God walks through the garden. Adam and Eve are hiding behind some bushes.

God: Where are you? Why are you hiding?

Adam: We're hiding because we don't have anything to wear.

Gen 3.9–14

Gen 2.15–17

There is a pause. A long, long, sad pause.

God: Who told you that? Have you eaten the fruit?

Adam: The woman made me do it!

Eve: The serpent made me do it!

Gen 3.14–21

And that is the end of Eden. The world is broken. Now they cannot stay in the garden, they cannot eat the fruit of the tree of life. From now on, Adam will fight the earth as he farms it; and Eve will cry in pain at childbirth; and the serpent – the serpent will be crushed, one day.

The man and woman are banished. But before they leave God gives them some clothes. In case they get cold.

I also sell double-glazing

Imagine what it was like for Adam and Eve; naming the animals, marvelling at the water and the light and the colours, exploring everything for the first time.

There was only one rule. Don't eat the fruit[1] of the tree of the knowledge of good and evil.

And what that meant was: who do you trust? Who do you allow to decide what is good and what is evil? Do you allow God to define what is right and wrong? Or do you want to decide yourself? That is what sin is, at its heart; it's putting our own desires first, choosing our moral code instead of God's.

Yet even having made this choice, God cannot stop loving them. He clothes them to face the cold. And the moment they rebel is the moment God puts his rescue plan into operation.

1 And we don't know what fruit it was. The Bible doesn't mention an apple. Personally I've always favoured the 'banana' theory, although there are many Old Testament scholars who plump for gooseberries.

1.4 Noah and the Flood

Years pass.

This is a time of long-livers, people with the air of Eden in their lungs. But the earth is full of evil. Sin has entered the world and it spreads like seeds on the wind. Adam and Eve's eldest son, Cain, kills his younger brother. Everywhere God looks, evil stains the earth. And there's only one thing to do with a stain: wash it clean.

Noah is a good man – perhaps the only good man on earth. God tells Noah to make a box, a huge, floating crate, with three floors. The job takes several years but when it is finished, God fills it with animals – two of every kind (and seven of some kinds). Noah, his wife, and their family go on board. In the dark, they listen as the rain starts to fall...

For forty days and forty nights it rains. The springs surge, the rivers rage until water covers the earth. They stay inside the ark for almost a year, until the waters begin to recede. Eventually, the ark comes to rest on top of a mountain called Ararat. And there, Noah and his family and all the animals emerge onto the damp earth, and Noah makes a sacrifice to God.

God promises that never again will he flood the earth in this way, and to seal his promise, he puts a rainbow in the sky.

After that, Noah invents wine.

Well, you've got to celebrate somehow.

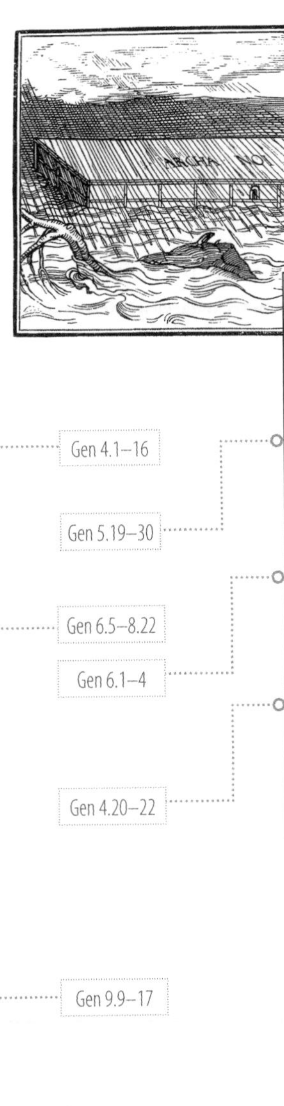

I don't want to worry you, but has anyone seen the woodworm recently?

This part of the Big Story is mysterious, unsettling.

Before the flood, the raw matter of creation still seems to hang in the air. People live for extraordinary lengths of time. Like Methuselah who lives, so they say, for nine hundred years. And his father Enoch whom God takes to be with him after 365 years. The Bible even tells us that there were giants walking the earth – the *Nephilim*, they are called. These great heroes are the offspring, so they say, of the sons of God and the daughters of men.

It is also a time of creativity and invention; Jubal invents music; Tubal-Cain invents metalwork; people build houses and cities.

Sadly, it is also a time of evil. The world has gone badly wrong. And God decides to wash it clean.[1] And after the flood, there comes the promise. These promises – or covenants – stud the Big Story like jewels. This is the first, a promise by God to Noah that never again will he flood the world. It is a contract, a solemn agreement.

And he signs it with a rainbow.

1 Scholars argue over the extent of the flood. Some believe it was truly a world-wide event; others that it covered 'the known world' as it were; that stretch of land covering ancient Mesopotamia. Some doubt it ever happened. Interestingly, however, there are accounts of a great, cataclysmic flood in other ancient mythologies from the area. The details differ in each account, but the dampness is common to all of them.

1.5 Babel and Abraham

Noah's sons become the ancestors of many different nations. And these nations multiply upon the earth, growing ever more powerful and ever more ambitious.

At one point they try to build a towering temple, so tall it will reach to God. So God reaches down and confuses their language, turns them into instant foreigners, so they can no longer understand one another.

So building ceases and, at Babel, men babble in different languages.

Many generations pass, then God chooses a man called Abram for the next part of the Big Story. He tells Abram to move to Canaan.

> God: I will give you the land. I will make your descendants into a mighty people. The whole world will be blessed because of them.

So Abram, his wife Sarai and their nephew Lot travel to Canaan. Eventually, Abram splits the territory with Lot. Lot selects the rich, green Jordan valley. Abram travels west, up the hills and into Canaan.

Gen 10

Gen 11.1–9

Gen 12.1–9

Gen 13.1–12

These two stories show different aspects of God's attitude to nationalities.

First there is the Babel episode, where men are coming together, but not for good. They are working together to try to beat God at his own game. Stupid. As the Big Story shows us, whenever men try to outsmart God it ends in tears.[1]

After men trying to be God, we see one man agreeing to follow God. When God disperses the nations, we see him starting one of his own. God chooses Abraham (or Abram as he was originally called) to start a special nation. This nation is to be the Israelites and Abraham is their headwater, their source.

Abraham is the Big Story's man of faith. God calls him and he responds, without knowing where he is going or what is going to happen. There are times in his life when he questions, there are times when his wife seems to be more in charge than he is. But when God calls him directly, there is always a positive response. In those times, Abraham is seen so clearly as the man of faith. Sometimes, when he has to decide for himself, he dithers. But when God tells him to move, he moves.

1 And quite frequently moans, whimpers and shouts of 'Oh boy, that hurts' as well.

It's bad news, I'm afraid. Our language is Welsh.

1.6 The Great Promise

Years pass. Abram and Sarai are old, with no sign of the promised descendants. Sarai suggests that Abram sleep with her maidservant Hagar. So Abram does and Hagar gets pregnant.

Both Hagar, and the situation, go pear-shaped. Sarai bullies Hagar so badly, she flees into the desert. There the Lord finds Hagar, weeping and alone.

God: Go back to your mistress. Your son, too, will be the father of a mighty nation.

So Hagar returns home and gives birth to a son. And she calls him Ishmael.

Still there is still no sign of a child for Abram and Sarai. Then, when Abram is 99 years old, the Lord promises Abram that he will have a son whose descendants will be kings. Abram (who is lying face down on the ground) starts giggling. How can such an old man and woman have a son? He suggests God use Ishmael, but God rejects this. Ishmael will be blessed, but it is Sarai's boy – Abram's second son – who will bear the blessing and the burden of God's promises.

God changes Abram's name to Abraham and Sarai's name to Sarah. And that day Abraham, Ishmael and all the men in their household are circumcised. (And the Jews have been circumcised ever since.)

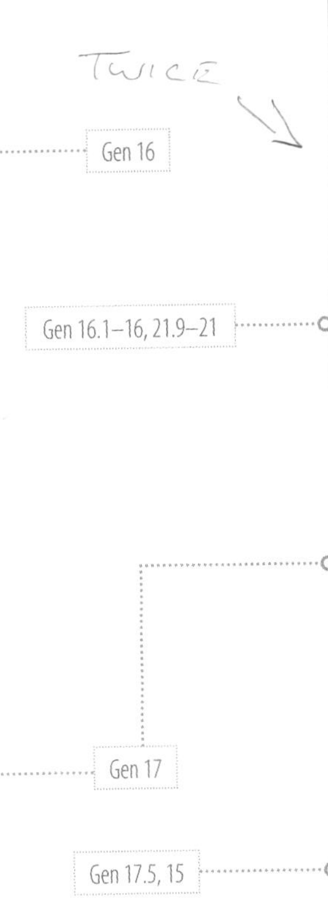

Sarah's attempt to engineer the fulfilment of God's promise drives Hagar out into the wilderness where she has a life-changing encounter. She meets God.

Hagar is fascinating. We don't know her background, we don't even know her real name,[1] but in the Big Story this simple, servant girl gets to meet God. Twice. Twice God rescues her; twice he comes to her aid. Even though the plan was stupid, God still cares for the people involved. He cares for Ishmael, whom God will also make into a mighty nation; he cares for Hagar, even though she is an Egyptian. God is the God of Israel, but he is also God of the whole world.

This 'wilderness encounter' is a key theme of the Big Story – but there are others here, too. There is the enduring promise that God makes to Abraham (as he had to Noah and will do to Jacob and David and others). He promises to be not only Abraham's God, but the God of his descendants.

Then there is the name change. Hagar is given a new name by her master. And then Abram is given a new name by his. Names are important in the Big Story. Names have power. Names define your character and the part you have to play.[2]

And another curious thing: it will be Abraham's *second* son who carries the promise forward, not Ishmael. The younger son. We'll be seeing more of him...

1 'Hagar' is not an Egyptian name, but she was from Egypt. So she was probably renamed when she entered service with Abraham.

2 Abraham means 'father of nations'.

1.7 Three Visitors

One hot summer afternoon, three visitors appear at Abraham's tent. He invites them in and cooks them a meal.

First mysterious figure: *(actually the Lord in disguise)* Where is Sarah?

Abraham: *(suddenly realising who he's talking to)* Over there.

First mysterious figure: I'll be back next year. And she will have borne a child.

Sarah (who is over ninety years old and listening to this conversation) bursts out laughing.

First mysterious figure: Why are you laughing? You think it's too difficult for me?

Sarah: *(from outside the tent)* I didn't laugh!

First mysterious figure: Yes you did.

Gen 18

When the meal is over, two of the visitors head towards Sodom and Gomorrah. The Lord, however, lingers a while, to tell Abraham of his plans to destroy Sodom and Gomorrah.

Abraham: Are you going to kill everyone, Lord? Good and bad? What if there are fifty good people the place?

God: If there are fifty I will spare the city.

Abraham: I have no right to ask this, but what if there are, say, forty-five?

God: If there are forty-five, I'll spare the city.

Abraham: Or forty?

God: If there are forty, I'll spare the city.

And so the conversation continues, with Abraham bargaining for the lives of the good people in Sodom. If there are any...

Meanwhile, the two others have reached Sodom, where Lot, Abraham's nephew, offers them hospitality. But a mob gathers. Lot tries to bargain with the mob, but fails to placate them. Then, suddenly he feels himself pulled back inside. The two 'men' have thrown off their disguise, taken off their sunglasses, rolled their sleeves up. They are pure power.

Lot and his family flee and the angels warn them not to look back. Behind them, the earth shatters; showers of sulphur spew out of the ground and the plain of Sodom and Gomorrah becomes a boiling, bubbling, molten furnace.

(Although she was told not to, Lot's wife looks back. She is caught in the hailstorm and turned into a pillar of salt.)

The next day, when Lot looks towards Sodom there is nothing there but smoke.

Gen 19

Did God really not know what was going on in Sodom? Did Abraham really change God's mind with his bartering?

Doubtful. What happens here is a gracious example of the friendship of God. As Abraham is his friend, God shares his plans and thoughts. He stays behind, lingers with his friends, shares their hospitality, tells them what he's going to do.[1]

There is justice, but it is not blind, unfeeling justice. It is not random, but specific; not based on a whim, but considered and, well, *just*.

And God, because he is friends with his creatures, because he is their Father, hangs around to explain things.

Is 1.9–10; Jer 49.18; Ezek 16.46–56; Amos 4.11; Mt 10.15; Rom 9.29; Rev 11.8

1 Talking of what he did, the fate of Sodom and Gomorrah becomes a big symbol for later prophets like Ezekiel, Jeremiah and even Jesus.

1.8 The Test of Abraham

God is true to his word. Sarah becomes pregnant and gives birth to Isaac. When he is eight days old, Abraham circumcises him as promised. And Sarah laughs – this time with joy.

Some years later, God speaks to Abraham.

God: Take the son whom you love and go to the region of Moriah. I want you to sacrifice him to me.

Abraham sets off. After three days they reach their destination and Abraham and Isaac climb the hill alone.

Isaac: We've got the wood and the knife, Father, but where is the animal?

Abraham: *(sadly)* God will provide something.

When they reach the summit, Abraham builds an altar and lays the wood on it. Then he grabs Isaac, ties him up and lays him on the wood.

The sunlight glints on the knife as it lifts into the air...

Angel of the Lord: Abraham! Abraham!

The voice comes out of nowhere.

Abraham: Here I am!

Angel of the Lord: Do not lay a hand on the boy. Now I know you fear God, because you are willing to sacrifice your only son.

Abraham turns round and sees a ram caught in a thicket. So he sacrifices that instead.

Then they go home.

Gen 21.1–8

Gen 22.1–18

One of the toughest parts of the Big Story. It is often given as evidence of Abraham's faith – that he was prepared to sacrifice his only son if that was what God wanted. Yet it seems like some cruel, bizarre practical joke. Why was God asking Abraham and Isaac to go through this? What kind of sadistic endurance test is this?

Certainly it was a test of faith. Abraham had been promised that he would be the father of a great nation, now God was apparently throwing all that away. And still he decided to do what God wanted, to give the most precious thing he owned back to God.

But even so, even so...

There is something deep going on here, some foretaste of the future, an event that lies at the very heart of the Big Story: the sacrifice of the son.

Gen 22.2; 2 Chr 3.1

The clue is in the location. Moriah was the place which was later to become Jerusalem. Jewish lore says that it was on Moriah that the temple was built. So maybe God is giving hints here. Perhaps he was pointing way forward, to a time when another Son would be sacrificed in Jerusalem. Only this time there would be no angel to stay the knife, no goat to take the boy's place.

Sacrifice is woven throughout the Big Story. People offer sacrifices in gratitude to God, but also to say 'sorry', to atone for their actions, to restore their relationship with God. This sacrifice on Mount Moriah is a forerunner of another sacrifice – the greatest sacrifice of all – and one which brings us all back to God.

MORIAH

But there's around two thousand years to go before that.

1.9 Jacob and Esau

Isaac grows up and marries Rebekah, who gives birth to twins. From the start the twins fight; – even in the womb they seem to jostle.

The eldest twin has thick red hair and he is called Esau. His younger brother comes out grasping his heel and he is called Jacob.

One day Esau returns from hunting absolutely famished. He finds Jacob cooking a lentil stew.

Esau: I'm starving.

Jacob: You can have some stew, but in exchange, I want your birthright.

Esau thinks about it, but not for long.

Esau: If I don't eat, I'll die and then it will be no use to me anyway. It's yours.

And with that he piles into the stew.

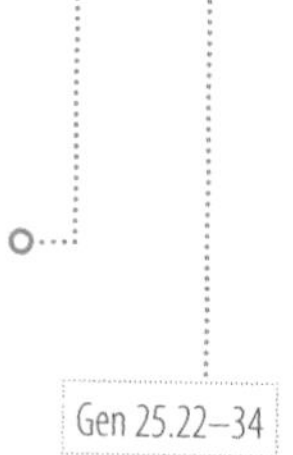

A few years on, Jacob pulls another, similar trick. Isaac, old and blind, is preparing to die. He wants to bless Esau, his first-born son. But these things have to be done properly, so he sends Esau out to hunt so they can share a meal.

Rebekah overhears this plan, so she tells Jacob to get two goats and make a stew up quickly. Then she takes the skins of the goats and ties them onto Jacob's neck and arms to disguise him as his hairier brother. Jacob goes to Isaac.

Jacob: Here I am, Father. It's Esau. I've prepared the stew for you.

Isaac: That was quick. How did you do that?

Jacob: The Lord granted me success.

Isaac feels Jacob's neck and hands; they are hairy, like Esau.

Isaac: You sound like Jacob, but feel like Esau. Are you really Esau?

Jacob: Of course.

Gen 27

So Isaac believes him and blesses him.

Isaac: Let nations serve you, let all your brothers bow down to you.

When Isaac finds out what has happened he trembles with fear. When Esau finds out he shakes with rage.

So Jacob decides to run away. Fast.

Gen 25.19–21

Jacob is the youngest of the twins born to Rebekah.[1] The younger son. I told you he'd be back. Here Jacob wins out over Esau (just as Isaac won out over Ishmael). Strangely, God blesses Jacob, despite the unfairness and trickery. It is as if that is what he has planned all along. Perhaps what is being reinforced here is that it is God's choice. That is what matters, not human notions of who is first in the pecking order.

Anyway, Jacob doesn't exactly win. This trickster has a voyage of discovery to go on. His trickery gains him the blessing, but he has to flee.

He loses everything and has to go on a journey.

And that's another theme entirely.

1 And Rebekah is barren; she only conceives as a result of prayer. Hmmm.

1.10 Jacob Wrestles God

On his journey, Jacob has a dream where he sees a ladder from earth to heaven, with angels ascending and descending. Right at the top is the Lord, who repeats the promise he gave to Jacob's grandfather, Abraham.

Jacob ends in Haran, working for his Uncle Laban. He marries two of Laban's daughters (he is tricked into marrying the eldest) and has many children, including twelve sons. Many years later, he and his family head back to Canaan. Scared that his brother might still be angry, he sends his wives and servants ahead with gifts. That night, Jacob is completely, utterly alone.

And in his loneliness, a stranger wrestles with Jacob. It takes all of Jacob's strength to hold on. At one point, the wrestler just reaches out a finger and dislocates Jacob's hip. Still Jacob does not let him go.

Jacob: I won't let you go unless you bless me.

Wrestler: What is your name?

Jacob: Jacob.

Wrestler: Not any more. You are now called Israel, because you have fought with God and men and not given in.

Then he blesses Jacob and disappears.

Jacob: I have seen the Lord face to face and I still live.

And with that he limps across the river to meet his brother.

Gen 28.10–22

Gen 29

Gen 31

Gen 32.1–32

Job 1.1–3, 2.1–10, 3.1–26, 38.1–42.17

Jacob's journey begins with a repetition of the promise given to his grandfather. Then the trickster is tricked, when he marries the wrong woman. He thinks he is marrying Rachel, but it is her sister Leah.[1]

And then there is the wrestling match.

Alone, afraid, completely isolated, Jacob has lost everything. Driven to prayer, in the middle of the night, he wrestles with God.

It is as if all the battles and struggles of Jacob's life were summed up in this match. Whatever he has been in the past, however he has behaved, he will not let God go. Jacob emerges broken, but blessed; limping but loved, defeated but strangely victorious. And he has a new name, a name that sums up his character: Israel.

Throughout the Big Story people enter the wilderness to encounter God. Indeed, one of the most profound wilderness encounters occurs somewhere around this time.

A wealthy, happy man called Job loses everything; friends, family, wealth, *everything*. He is a good person. Why has this happened to him? As he sits on a rubbish dump outside town, he 'wrestles' with God, trying to comprehend the purpose and nature of suffering. His questions are stilled, in the end, by a personal encounter with God himself; leading to new blessings and a new life, and, maybe, a new understanding.

I don't suppose there's any chance of installing a lift?

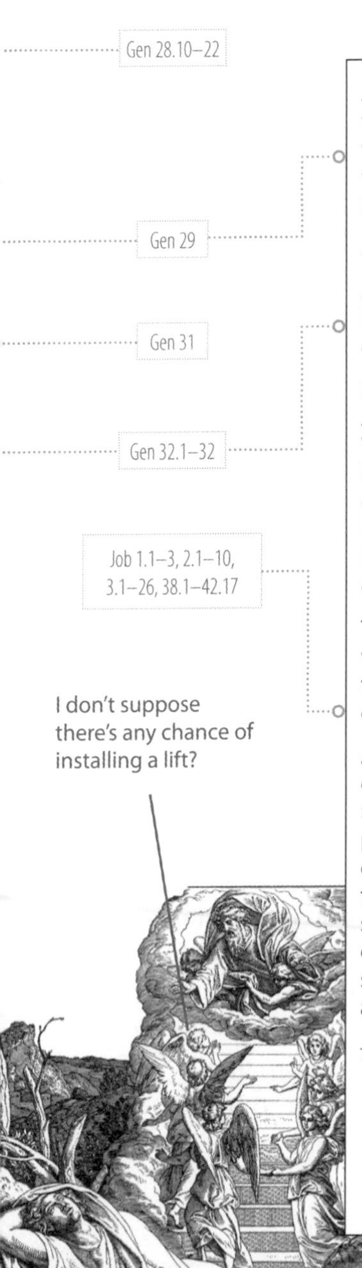

1 Jacob didn't know who he was marrying because his bride was entirely veiled, with only the eyes showing. One feels for the unwanted, unmarriageable Leah, but, as with Hagar, God has compassion on her – she becomes the mother of half of all Jacob's sons, while Rachel struggles to conceive. Jacob gets his own back on his uncle, when he increases his own flocks by a cunning scheme of early genetic engineering.

1.11 Joseph

Joseph is Jacob's favourite son.

But his brothers hate Joseph with a passion. They hate the way he sneaks on them to his father. They hate the fact that Jacob gives Joseph a wonderful, richly embroidered robe. And they hate his dreams – dreams which foretell that one day they will bow down to him. Gen 37

So they get rid of him. They throw him down a well and fake his death. They sell him as a slave, smear his robe with goat's blood, and tell Jacob his favourite son is dead. Jacob's heart is broken.

Joseph is taken to Egypt, where he becomes a trusted slave in a posh household – until while refusing the advances of the lady of the house, he is accused of attempted rape and thrown into prison. There, he meets a baker and a cup-bearer who once worked for Pharaoh. They have vivid dreams which Joseph interprets. His interpretations prove to be correct and, two years later, when Pharaoh has some mysterious dreams the cup-bearer (who has been restored to his post) recommends Joseph.

Joseph is fetched from the jail and interprets the dreams as predicting a famine for Egypt. Pharaoh is so impressed he appoints Joseph – the dreamer – as his second-in-command. Gen 39–46

Seven years later, the famine hits Canaan. So Jacob sends his sons down to Egypt to buy grain. When the brothers get there, they are granted an audience with an Egyptian official called Lord Zaphenath–Paneah. What they don't know is that his real name is Joseph.

Joseph teases his brothers, accusing them of spying. Eventually, however, he can bear the pretence no more and he tells them the truth. The brothers are reconciled and reunited. The aged Jacob is brought to Egypt to be reunited with his long-lost son.

The descendants of Jacob and his sons remain in Egypt for many years. Centuries, in fact. There, they multiply, until there are so many of them they could hardly be counted. They are organised into twelve great families, or tribes, each descended from the twelve sons of Jacob.

Or as God called him, 'Israel'.

Ex 1.1–7

The tribes of Israel are descended from Jacob's sons.[1] And they end this act in Egypt, brought there by the brother they thought they'd killed. Once again, we see a person lose everything before they can find themselves. Joseph's pride and boastful behaviour results in him losing everything; his family, his home, his very identity. Yet by doing that and turning to God, he finds who he truly is and what part he should play in God's plans.

More, we see someone come back from the dead. Death and rebirth; happens a lot in the Big Story. Joseph was 'missing presumed dead', but God gives him life and meaning and purpose.

Gen 48.1–22

(By the way, Joseph has two sons. On his deathbed, Jacob, Joseph's father blesses the younger son, Ephraim, over the older son, Manasseh. Now, where have I seen that before?)

Gen 35.23–26; Ex 1.2–5; Num 1.20–43; 1 Chr 2.1–2; Rev 7.5–8

1 There are different lists of the tribes in different parts of the Bible, but the generally accepted list is: Simeon, Levi, Judah, Issachar, Zebulun, Benjamin, Dan, Naphtali, Gad, Asher, Ephraim and Manasseh.

Act 2
The Exodus

In which we see Moses lead the Israelite nation out of slavery in Egypt; witness their disobedience to God at Mount Sinai; wander with them for forty years in the wilderness and eventually see them arrive at and inhabit the promised land of Canaan.

ACT 2: THE EXODUS

2.1	Moses on the Nile
2.2	The Burning Bush
2.3	A Plague on you
2.4	The Law and the Calf
2.5	The Wilderness
2.6	The Judges
2.7	Ruth

CAST

Moses	Rescuer of the enslaved Israelites
Aaron	His brother and spokesman
Pharaoh	A stupid Egyptian leader
Joshua	Moses' PA and successor as leader
Caleb	A faithful spy
Deborah	A female judge
Gideon	Another judge
Samson	A big strong, hairy judge

Various moaning Israelites,
soldiers, Egyptians, Amalekites,
Philistines, minor judges, etc.

2.1 Moses on the Nile

The Nile rises, the Nile falls; centuries pass, and the Israelites (as they are now known) grow ever more numerous. There are Pharaohs now who do not remember Joseph and they turn the Israelites into slaves. But so populous are the Israelites that Pharaoh orders a cull.

Pharaoh: Throw every Hebrew baby boy into the Nile. But you can let the girls live.

Oh, the sorrow of those slaves; the weeping of those mothers. One mother takes her baby, puts him into a basket and sets him afloat to take his chances on the Nile. A little way down-stream Pharaoh's daughter is bathing. She sees the basket and inside she finds the crying baby. Instantly her heart goes out to him.

A bystander – actually the baby's elder sister – volunteers to go and find a nurse for the baby, and she chooses the baby's real mother! Pharaoh's daughter takes him into her household. And she calls him Moses.

One day Moses sees an Egyptian master beating a Hebrew slave. Angry, he kills the bully and buries the body. His crime, however, is discovered and he has to flee into the desert. There, he works as a shepherd. He marries a Midianite woman called Zipporah. He spends many years working in the desert while, all the time, the Israelites' suffering increase.

Ex 2.11–25

Ex 1

Ex 2.1–10

At the beginning of this part of the Big Story, the Israelites are enslaved in Egypt. Centuries have passed and the success of Joseph has been forgotten. Now Abraham's descendants are enslaved and abused.

When you view people as less than human, you can do what you want to them; put them to work in appalling conditions; treat them like cattle; *cull* them.

At the start of his story, Moses follows the pattern of many of his predecessors; he loses everything, becomes a nobody. He floats up the Nile in a box.[1] Like Jacob and Joseph he loses his identity, takes on a different name. Moses is the short version of an Egyptian name, stemming from the Egyptian verb meaning 'to give birth'.[2]

(Another interesting thing, Moses was not the first-born of the family, his brother Aaron was three years older. Younger son again...)

Anyway, you can take the boy out of the Hebrews, but you can't take the Hebrew out of the man. His mother had obviously taught him about his background and when he sees abuse happening, something snaps.

And so, this Egyptian prince loses everything and is driven into the desert. And we all know what happens there...

And this one even comes with its own presentation box.

1 Interestingly, the Hebrew word here is *teba* which means, apparently 'box-shaped thing'. That'd be a box, then. It's the same word used for Noah's boat and the only other time that the word is used in the Old Testament. So there is a connection straight away between Moses and Noah. Well I thought it was interesting...

2 E.g. Rameses, meaning 'Re is born'. 'Re' or 'Ra' was the Egyptian sun god. What do you mean you're *still* not interested?

2.2 The Burning Bush

Moses is tending the sheep, as usual, in the desert, when in the distance he sees a fire. As he approaches he sees that it is a bush; yet, although the fire leaps and courses through the branches, the bush remains whole.

As he approaches the bush, God calls to him from within the fire.

God: Take off your shoes. This ground is holy. I am the God of your fathers – of Abraham and Isaac and Jacob. I have seen the misery of my people in Egypt and I want to rescue them. I want you to go and tell Pharaoh to release them. Don't worry, I will be with you.

Moses: Yes, but who are you?

The fire roars and crackles.

God: I AM WHO I AM! Tell them that. Tell them I AM has sent you!

Moses is alarmed by this task. A poor speaker, he asks God for help.

God: Your brother. Aaron the Levite; he speaks well. He will speak for you.

So Moses returns to Egypt and he and Aaron go to Pharaoh and order him to release the Israelites. Pharaoh refuses. Instead he makes the Israelite slaves work twice as hard.

Moaning Israelites: Things were bad enough before you two arrived. Now you've made Pharaoh hate us even more!

Moses: Even my own people don't believe me! What hope have I got with Pharaoh?

Another desert encounter with God.

And more names. As we have already seen, to name someone was to have ownership over them. Pharaoh, for example, had an official name and a secret name; and he kept his secret name, well, secret. It was believed that if others discovered his secret name, they would have control over him.

Ex 3

Here God does exactly the opposite. While to us it may sound as though he was trying to avoid giving out his name, that's not the case; he was telling Moses exactly who he was. Or is, rather. Or will be...

Because the name he gives expresses totality. God just is. Always has been, always will be. We're reminded of where we started, with a Being outside time, always present and always in the present tense.

Ex 4.10–17

So several themes merge here. The names, yes, but also the lingering, patient friendship of God. Did God have to explain anything to Moses? Did he have to persuade him, help him, give him Aaron as a spokesman? No, not really. But he chose to.

Above all it introduces the theme of rescue. God has seen his people in trouble and he will rescue them.

Ex 5

So Moses goes back to Egypt, helped by his brother Aaron and tells the Israelites who he is and what he's come to do. They are underwhelmed, to say the least. Their gripes and moans are a sign of things to come; when you read of their reactions to God's rescue plan, it's hard to escape the conclusion that these were the least grateful freed slaves ever.

2.3 A Plague on You

Pharaoh refuses Moses' request. He will not let the Israelites go. So, one morning, while Pharaoh is walking by the Nile, Moses stretches out his hand over the river. Immediately the water turns to blood. The fish die, the smell is awful. But Pharaoh does not let the people go.

A week passes. Then God sends another plague: millions of frogs emerge from the crimson waters, invading the houses, covering the beds. Pharaoh agrees to let the people go, but then changes his mind. So God sends a series of plagues, a terrible, escalating punishment on the gods of Egypt. Clouds of gnats that choke like dust; the livestock dies; festering boils break out on the bodies of men and animals; a terrible hailstorm destroys the crops and strips the trees; a huge swarm of locusts devours what little is left after the hailstorm; then a deep, deathly darkness completely covers the land.

In the face of these Pharaoh sometimes agrees to release the Israelites, but somehow he always changes his mind.

So, God decides to send one final, terrible plague. At midnight he will pass over the land, and the eldest sons of the Egyptians will die (and the eldest offspring of their livestock as well). Ex 11

The Israelites must protect themselves from this onslaught; they must smear lambs' blood on the doorposts of their houses – wherever he sees the blood, the angel of death will pass over. Ex 12

Rich and poor, high-born and low, all lose their eldest sons. By morning there is nowhere free from mourning. Pharaoh summons Moses and tells him to leave and never come back.

So Moses leads the people out of Egypt. By day God leads them with a pillar of cloud and by night with a pillar of fire.

But Pharaoh sends his chariots after them and they catch the Israelites by the Sea of Reeds. The Lord parts the sea and the Israelites walk across between walls of water. When the Egyptian chariots follow, the walls collapse and the entire army drowns.

Ex 7–10

The people see the power of the Lord and put their trust in him and in his servant Moses.

Ex 13–14

For now, anyway...

The plagues are more than God 'persuading' a recalcitrant Pharaoh; each plague is a comment on one of the Egyptian gods. They had gods who were flies, frogs, the sun; even the Nile was viewed as a god. So the *real* God shows who is actually in charge of the frogs and the flies; he overcomes the sun-god by bringing darkness; he overwhelms the Nile-god by turning it to blood. Pharaoh, too, was seen as a god in human form and he (or a predecessor at least) decided to kill the baby boys of the Israelites. Now God inflicts a similar punishment and Pharaoh, the all-powerful 'god', is powerless to do anything about it.

Ex 12.2; Lev 23.5; Lk 22.7–20

And there's Passover. A defining event for the Israelites and one that is celebrated to this day; it celebrates God's rescue,[1] reminds them of the enduring strength of God's promise. From now on the Israelite calendar year starts here, with this new beginning. We shall see this 'new start' again in the Big Story, only changed, transformed, made into a new celebration of a new promise, an even greater rescue.

1 Talking of rescue, it was the 'Sea of Reeds' (Hebrew *Yam Suph*) that the Israelites crossed. Since reeds don't grow in salt water that would make it an inland water, not the Red Sea as is commonly supposed. No, don't thank me, I'm just doing my job.

2.4 The Law and the Calf

In the desert, the Lord sends his people quail to eat, and manna (a kind of bread which appears each morning in thin flakes, like frost on the ground). He even provides fresh water from a rock. Even so, the people grumble.

Three months after leaving Egypt, they come to Mount Sinai. God descends in a dense cloud and he calls Moses up to him. God gives Moses the law by which he wants the Israelites to live.

Down at the bottom of the mountain, the people think that Moses isn't ever coming back. They persuade Aaron to build them a new god, a calf made out of gold.

When God sees this betrayal he decides to destroy them. But Moses pleads for the people. He rushes down the mountain and mashes up the golden calf. The Levite tribe pass through the camp, quelling the riot by force.

The Lord is angry with the Israelites; but he is pleased with Moses. As a reward, he allows Moses to see him. Well, a bit of him.

> God: You can't see my face. No-one can see my face and live.

Moses climbs the mountain with two new, blank, stone tablets (the originals were destroyed in the riot). And he sees the back of God. When he returns his face is glowing because he has seen the Lord. So radiant is his face that he has to cover it with a veil.

He puts the tablets in the Ark of the Covenant.

Ex 16

Ex 17.1–7

Ex 19.1–20.21

Ex 32.1–14, 26–28

Ex 33.17–34.35, 40.16–21

At the mountain where he saw the burning bush, Moses meets God again. This time God gives him the law, the rules by which the Israelites must live. At its heart are the Ten Commandments, but it also encompasses social behaviour, hygiene, food, religious observance – the whole range of Israelite life.

It also includes detailed instructions on religious ritual. Moses is told how to build the Ark of the Covenant (a box to hold the tablets on which the law has been engraved) and the Tabernacle (a kind of portable, flat-pack temple). If they break the laws the Israelites must offer sacrifices, to atone for their sins. And there is also social legislation; laws which guide their treatment of foreigners, slaves and the poor. This is their guide to how to live, their 'how to be holy.'

Trouble is, the people haven't quite grasped this whole 'holiness' thing. While Moses is up the mountain hearing the truth, the Israelites are down at the bottom, creating a lie. Unbelievably, only a few weeks out of Egypt, having seen all that they'd seen, they create a fake god.

Moses descends, destroys the idol and punishes the wrongdoers.[1] The reward for his faithfulness is being allowed to see God. Or his back, at least. In doing so, he is exposed to raw, undiluted holiness. It makes him glow. What God touches is so holy it burns.[2]

This is why obedience is so important. This is why doing things right *matters*. God is a dangerous substance.

1 The idolaters are punished by the Levites (Moses's own tribe) which marks the start of their special service to God as the priestly tribe.

2 It happens as well with the Ark of the Covenant. If handled wrongly, the holiness in the box just spills out, destroying any unholy people near it.

Of course I'm a god – I moo in a mysterious way

2.5 The Wilderness

Soon, the Israelites reach the borders of Canaan, the land God has promised them. Moses sends twelve spies into the land and when they return, the spies are distraught.

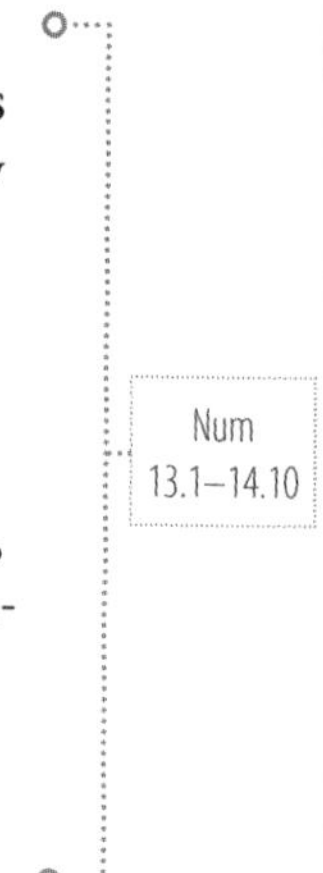

> Spies: The land is full of wonderful produce. But the people are huge! They would beat us to a pulp. We cannot defeat them.

Only Caleb and Joshua disagree. Nevertheless, rumours about the inhabitants spread throughout the Israelite camp, and the people believe that there are giants in the land.

> Moaning Israelites: We're like insects compared to them!

They refuse to enter the land and even threaten to stone Moses and Aaron.

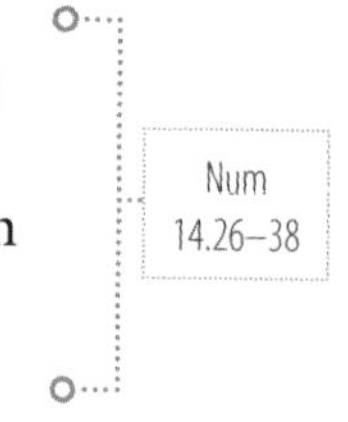

God is so angry at their lack of faith he threatens to destroy them and start again, but Moses pleads for forgiveness. Even so, God decides that none of this scared, disbelieving generation will see the Promised Land – except Caleb and Joshua. Instead the people are forced to spend forty years wandering in the wilderness. Along the way, they also face opposition from other nations, but the Lord brings them victory each time.

Eventually, the faithless generation who left Egypt die; the Israelites return to the borders of the promised land. Moses stands on Mount Nebo, and looks down across the Jordan to the Promised Land. He too will not be allowed to

I'm playing a tuba of mass destruction.

enter. He can look, but he can't touch. Then Moses dies and is buried in a place that remains unknown to this day. Deut 34.5–7

So it is Joshua who leads the Israelites into the land that God has given them. They conquer many towns and cities (including Jericho, where the walls collapse) and many armies (such as the Amalekites, where God keeps the sun standing still so they can fight longer). Num 27.12–22; Josh 1 Josh 5.13–6.27, 10.1–15

The land is conquered: job done. Except that it isn't. The Israelites don't finish the job. Although the Israelites occupy the land (which is divided up between the twelve tribes) many small cities and outposts remain unconquered, filled with Canaanites worshipping Canaanite gods. Josh 13.1–7; Judg 1.21, 27–35

And, over the next few centuries, these gods were to prove very tempting to the Israelites.

It is their lack of faith, and their failure to obey God's instructions, which bar the Israelites from the promised land. Even Moses trips up; at one point he fails to follow God's exact instructions and God bars him from entering.[1]

The Israelites' part of the big promise was to obey God, to follow his laws, but time and again they fail. Even when they are in the Promised Land, they don't manage it. God instructs them to purge the place, to cleanse it of all the foreign gods, to disinfect it of all the heathen worship of the Canaanites.

But they do not finish the job. Once they have the land, they relax, leaving certain cities unconquered. Which is why it all goes wrong.

1 This seems very hard on Moses. However we should note, he made it there in the end, in a meeting with Jesus and Elijah. Mt 17.1–9

2.6 The Judges

After Joshua dies, the land descends into a time of chaos, darkness and depravity; a time where everyone does as he wants.

It is the time of the judges.

Throughout these years the same pattern loops around. The people of Israel turn to the gods of the other nations. Disaster falls on them, they repent and cry out to God, and he sends someone to rescue them. They are very grateful, and worship him. Then they start to look around them at the gods of other nations... and the tape loop goes round again.

Judg 2.16–19

Their rescuers are the 'judges'. As well as famous judges like Deborah (who leads Israel to victory over a Canaanite army) and Gideon, (who defeats the Midianites with only three hundred men), there are shadowy figures like Tola, Shamgar, and Ehud, the left-handed assassin, who kills King Eglon of Moab. (Eglon is so obese that when Ehud stabs him, the King's stomach-fat closes over the hilt and Ehud can't get the sword out again.)

Judg 4–5

Judg 6.11–8.35

Judg 3.11–31, 10.1–2

And then there is Samson. Samson is a Nazirite, a sect who never cut their hair or touch alcohol. Prodigiously strong, he has a fatal flaw: women. Samson cannot resist a pretty face, especially if there is a nice body attached. He makes a disastrous marriage with a Philistine woman. When the marriage collapses, the Philistines attack

Num 6.1–21; Judg 13.1–25

Judg 14–15

Samson, but he kills a thousand of them armed with only a donkey's jawbone.

Then he falls in love with a Philistine prostitute called Delilah. She coaxes out of Samson the secret of his strength; he never cuts it. If the hair's long, he's strong; if it's short, he's caught. So, while he is sleeping one day, she shaves his head. The Philistines burst in; Samson rises to fight, but finds his strength gone. The Philistines capture him, gouge his eyes out and set him on a treadmill, grinding corn.

Judg 16

In the darkness, his hair begins to grow again...

One day the Philistines hold a feast in the great temple of Dagon. As the entertainment they bring out the blind, chained Samson. Surrounded by the jeers and catcalls, Samson gropes his way to the two massive, central pillars. He prays to God for just enough strength for one last push... He pushes. The pillars creak, the mortar cracks, the roof of the temple collapses, killing everyone inside.

It is Samson's greatest triumph. And his tomb.

The time of the judges shows what happens in a world without God. Back to choices; each man doing his own thing, each person eating the fruit of the knowledge of good and evil.

It is a time of compromise; a time when even heroes are badly flawed. Samson,[1] with his love of women; Gideon who at the end worships the false gods of everyone else. People start well and finish poorly; people make dumb choices. But that's what happens when there is no king and everyone does what he wants.

1 His mother was barren and unable to have children, but then an angel appeared to her and told her she would have a son. Hmmm...

Judg 13.2–24

2.7 Ruth

Around the time of the judges there is an Israelite woman called Naomi. When a famine hits Israel, she and her husband move to Moab – a nation which usually wars with Israel. There, her two sons marry Moabite women. Sadly Naomi's husband dies, as do her sons. Poor and lost, she decides to return to her home near Bethlehem.

She expects her two daughters-in-law to remain in Moab, but one of them, called Ruth, decides to follow Naomi.

> Ruth: I'll go with you.
>
> Naomi: Shouldn't you stay with your people?
>
> Ruth: Your people are my people. And your God, my God.

They return to Bethlehem and there Ruth begins to work in the harvest fields. Soon, she is noticed by Boaz, a prosperous farmer and relative of Naomi. Boaz is impressed by Ruth's devotion and offers her protection.

She shows him love and he loves her in return.

Boaz goes to the elders and he redeems the land that was once owned by Naomi's dead husband. And that gives him the right to marry Ruth.

So Ruth and Boaz marry. Later they have a child, Obed.

And he is the grandfather of King David.

Ruth 1–4

In the dark time of the judges, this tiny love story shines out.

Ruth is not an Israelite; she's from Moab. But she is the one in this tale who embodies selfless love and devotion. It's not about where you come from; it's about obeying and loving God.

In her selfless love for Naomi, Ruth echoes the faithful love of God for his people. And in rescuing Ruth and Naomi from poverty, Boaz embodies another key Big Story theme: redemption.[1] Redemption means buying someone's freedom; purchasing a relative from slavery.

And this redeeming love leads to David who will rescue Israel and make it great – and even further, to the one who will save all people from eternal slavery.

In the heart of the dark time of the judges, this story points ahead, to the perfect love which banishes all darkness.

Mt 1.5–6

No wonder Ruth is honoured; no wonder this outsider, this foreigner gets a mention in the family tree of Christ.

What's a nice girl like you doing in a field like this?

1 The word occurs twenty-three times in the book. Really. Not that I've counted...

Act 3
The Kings

In which we see the establishment of a monarchy in Israel; watch a civil war split the country into two kingdoms of Israel and Judah; witness the destruction of Israel; and see the exile and eventual return of Judah.

ACT 3: THE KINGS

3.1	King Saul
3.2	David and Goliath
3.3	David becomes King
3.4	David and Bathsheba
3.5	Absalom Rebels
3.6	Solomon the Wise
3.7	The Divided Kingdom
3.8	Elijah
3.9	Elijah on the Mountain
3.10	Elisha and Beyond
3.11	The End of Israel
3.12	The End of Judah
3.13	Exile
3.14	Return

CAST

Samuel	A judge and prophet
Saul	First king of Israel
Jonathan	His son
David	Second king of Israel
Absalom	His rebellious son
Solomon	Third king of Israel. Wise man.
Rehoboam	First king of Judah
Jeroboam	First king of Israel (Northern Kingdom)
Elijah	Great prophet
Elisha	Another great prophet
Isaiah Jeremiah Daniel Ezekiel	Later prophets
Nebuchadnezzar	A Babylonian emperor
Cyrus	Emperor of the Persians
Esther	A Jewish girl and Persian queen
Ezra Nehemiah	Leaders who take exiles home

Also, various good and bad kings (mostly bad), invading armies, minor prophets, etc.

3.1 King Saul

Israel is in a terrible state. Without leadership, with a corrupt priesthood, constantly under attack by the Philistines (who at one stage even capture the ark of the covenant) the people want stability.

So they go to Samuel, a prophet who has been dedicated to the Lord from an early age. They ask Samuel for a king, but Samuel reports that God is against the idea.

God: *(via Samuel)* A king will take your sons for his army and your daughters for his servants. He will take ten per cent of your vineyards and olive groves and your flocks and you will even become his slaves.

Moaning Israelites: We don't care. We want a king like all the other nations have...

So, in the end, God agrees. He leads Samuel to Saul, a boy from the tribe of Benjamin. Saul becomes the first king of Israel.

He starts well. He defeats the Ammonites and he has the Spirit of God in him.

But soon cracks appear. He is headstrong, impatient, disobedient. Rather than doing things as God wants, he takes things into his own hands. He makes silly decisions.

So in the end, the Lord rejects Saul as king and Samuel begins to search for his successor.

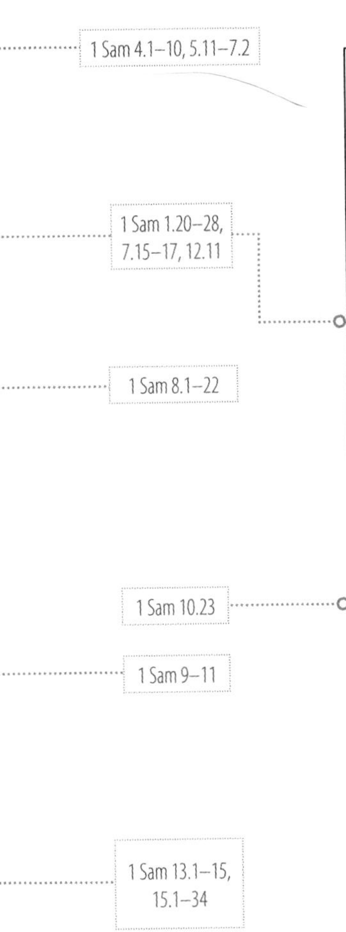

Is God a republican? Certainly he never wanted his people to have a king. He wanted them to obey him. But they were looking at what the other nations had and they wanted the same. Keeping up with the Joneses. Or keeping up with the Philistines, to be more precise.

So they ask for a king, and the person they ask is Samuel, a prophet and the last of the judges. Samuel was an unexpected child, born as the result of prayer and dedicated to God from an early age. He becomes the figure who anoints the first kings of Israel.

Anyway, God reluctantly grants the Israelites their request and leads Samuel to a lad called Saul; tall, strong and showing potential.[1]

Sadly, potential was all Saul ever really showed. Although he was, literally, head and shoulders above the rest, in other ways he proved to be less outstanding. His main failing was that he couldn't obey God.

We're back at the need for exact obedience; for precision in walking the path laid out by God. But Saul was always trying to push God along, to change the instructions, to engineer God's success.

He simply doesn't obey. Israel's first ever king is a failure.

Well, you can't blame God. He did try to warn them.

1 The name Saul comes from the Hebrew meaning 'the one asked for, requested.'

3.2 David and Goliath

Samuel finds the next king in Bethlehem.

The youngest son of a man called Jesse (who is the grandson of Ruth and Boaz), David is a shepherd, but also a talented musician and poet. He first comes to prominence when he joins Saul's court. Saul, who is increasingly paranoid, finds David's music soothing.

1 Sam 16.1–31

But it is the arrival of Goliath that propels David to fame.

The Philistines invade again and they have on their side a giant Philistine warrior called Goliath – about nine foot tall and built like a brick temple. Every morning Goliath challenges the Israelites to fight him; strangely no-one takes him up on this.

David, who has come to the Israelite camp to deliver some food for his brothers, can't understand why no-one is standing up to this man.

> David: I'll fight him. As a shepherd I've fought lions and bears; the Lord will deliver me from this beast as well.

So David fights Goliath. He is too small to wear the king's armour, but it doesn't matter; what he lacks in strength he makes up for in accuracy. Using a sling and a small pebble, he shoots Goliath in the head. The Philistines flee in chaos and David becomes a hero.

Which does not go down well with Saul.

That'll smart a bit.

David is one of the great heroes of the Bible. He comes from humble beginnings – a lad working as a shepherd near the small town of Bethlehem. Although Jesse has eight sons, it is David, the youngest, whom God chooses.[1]

Just as God chose Abraham to father the nation, so he chooses David to be the father of kings. And, like Abraham, David is characterised by his faith.

He was a talented musician, and a great poet (read his Psalms) but what marked him out was his willingness to trust God. Samuel described David as 'a man after God's own heart.' That's what made him a great king. He wanted what God wanted.

1 Sam 17

1 Sam 13.14

It is this that is at the root of his most famous victory. David v. Goliath is often cited as a case of victory for the underdog, but that wasn't how David saw it. In David's eyes he was simply obeying God. As far as he could see Goliath hadn't got a chance.

It's not that he wasn't brave – you've got to have guts to stand up to giants. But his bravery was backed up by seeing God at work. God had already supported him in battles with bears and lions, so why should a nine-foot high Philistine be any problem?

1 A king born in Bethlehem. Store that away, it might come in useful later.

3.3 David Becomes King

Saul's envy of David's popularity descends into paranoia. He wants to kill him, even though David is now married to his daughter and is close friends with his son, Jonathan. One night, Saul throws a spear at David, but it misses. Jonathan warns David that his house is being watched, and David flees to Ramah.

1 Sam 18–20

David becomes a guerilla warrior, hiding in caves, scavenging for food. At one point he even lives among the Philistines, where to escape revenge for killing Goliath, he pretends to be mad. Twice he has the opportunity to kill Saul, but he refuses; despite his behaviour, Saul is still the anointed king.

1 Sam 21.10–15

1 Sam 24–26

Then Saul's attention is diverted from hunting David, because the Philistines invade (again). Saul is terrified. He wants to ask Samuel for help, but Samuel is dead. So, in disguise, Saul visits a witch. She conjures up the spirit of Samuel who, far from comforting the king, tells Saul he is doomed.

1 Sam 28

Saul fights the Philistines on the slopes of Mount Gilboa. There he and his son, Jonathan, are slain. Some say that, facing imminent defeat, he orders his servant to kill him; others that Saul takes his own life. Whatever the case, the Philistines find the bodies of Saul and his sons, cut off their heads, and fasten their bodies to the walls of Beth Shan.

1 Sam 31

Their bodies are retrieved by men from Jabesh Gilead. And when David hears what has happened he mourns bitterly for Saul and for Jonathan.

1 Sam 31.8–13; 2 Sam 1.1–2.7

There is a period of civil war in Israel, with Saul's son Ish-Bosheth supported by the northern tribes. Eventually, Ish-Bosheth is assassinated by two of his own followers and David becomes king over all Israel.

2 Sam 2

2 Sam 4

One of his first acts is to capture Jerusalem. Up till now it has been owned by the Canaanite tribe of the Jebusites. David takes the city by sending troops up through a water-tunnel and, over the next few years, he turns Jerusalem into a magnificent capital. He brings the Ark of the Covenant into the city and is so excited that he throws off all his clothes and dances in his underwear (much to the disgust of his wife).

2 Sam 5.6–12

2 Sam 6

He defeats and subdues the Philistines, the Arameans, the Moabites, Ammonites and all the nations surrounding Israel. He composes wonderful poetry and even starts planning a magnificent temple to the Lord, to be built in Jerusalem.

2 Sam 8.1–14

2 Sam 22

2 Sam 7.1–17; 1 Chr 17.1–15

God sends the prophet Nathan with a message:

> God: Your house and throne will last forever.

2 Sam 7.16

It is all going fantastically well.

Saul's hatred for David drives him into exile, but David remains faithful to God. Given the chance to kill Saul he refuses. He will not try to force God's hand. David's future is up to God.

And, of course, God does deliver the kingdom to David. David establishes the capital at Jerusalem and God makes a covenant with David; his family, his 'throne' will last forever. The promise again; the guarantee.

3.4 David and Bathsheba

It is spring. The time when kings go off to war.

Only not this time. David, perhaps needing a rest after years of conflict, is in his palace, while his army is off fighting the Ammonites.

One evening, David cannot sleep. He goes onto the roof of his palace to get some fresh air. As he looks down at the city, he sees a woman bathing, and immediately falls head over heels in lust. He sends for her and she sleeps with him that night. Her name is Bathsheba and she is married to Uriah the Hittite – one of David's commanders.

Then she gets pregnant. David, the great, brave warrior, panics. He recalls Uriah from the front and tries to persuade him to sleep with his wife. But Uriah has no intention of spending a night in comfort when his troops are unable to do the same, so David's alibi is ruined. 2 Sam 11

When Uriah returns to the war, David issues instructions to his trusted commander Joab.

> David: Put Uriah where the fighting is heaviest. Then pull the rest of the troops back.

The plan works. Under the walls of Rabbah, Uriah is killed. The enemy strikes the blow, but it is David's hand which kills him.

Bathsheba mourns for her husband. But she marries David and bears him a son.

So far, so undetected. But the Lord has seen everything. And he sends the prophet Nathan to confront David. Nathan tells David a story about a rich man who stole a poor man's only sheep – even though he has many sheep of his own. David, angry at the injustice, vows that the rich man should be punished. Then the truth dawns on him...

Nathan tells David that, because of his sin, conflict will always be a part of his family and household; and that the son Bathsheba has born will die.

David is heartbroken with remorse. He prays with all his might. He refuses to eat. He pleads with God. But the child dies.

In due time, Bathsheba bears David another son. And they call him Solomon.

Difficult to stay disciplined in a palace. Difficult to stay faithful when your life is full of feasts. In his fights with Saul, his battles against the Philistines, David had relied on God. But when he's got the city, the palace, the throne, the promise of God's enduring love forever...

We've seen the importance of obedience, now we see the consequences of disobedience. We see what happens when you relax.

It is a story that reveals the truth, a story that acts as a mirror to David, that shows him the truth about his grievous, grubby, shabby, shameful sin. When confronted, David doesn't argue, doesn't try to justify his sin. Instead he weeps and prays.

This is David's wilderness moment. This is the crunch. Painful, tragic as it was, it leads him to a new relationship with God. His sin had tragic, inevitable, far-reaching consequences. It left the mighty king a lonely, lost, forlorn figure. But it also led him to the arms of a loving, forgiving God.

3.5 Absalom Rebels

Nathan's prediction about David's family proves true. They are appalling. One of his sons rapes one of David's daughters. And then there is Absalom. Absalom is David's son. He has good looks, popularity, a cruel savage streak and an ego the size of Mount Sinai. Soon the inevitable happens: he rebels against his father.

In the battle near the Forest of Ephraim, Absalom's army is slaughtered. Absalom tries to escape, but his head gets caught up in the thick branches of an oak; he is left hanging in mid-air while his mule keeps going. As the prince hangs there, Joab, David's brutal army captain, cold-bloodedly drives three javelins into him.

When David hears of the death of his son he is devastated. He hides in a room, weeping, until Joab forces him to pull himself together.

All this blood...

In the end the King grows old, and whatever he does he cannot get warm.

He always wanted to build a temple to the Lord, but God tells him he can't. There is too much blood on his hands. On his deathbed, David promises the kingship should pass to Solomon.

Then David dies and is buried in Jerusalem, the city he loved. And even to this day it is known as the City of David.

2 Sam 13.1–19

In the latter half of his reign, David seems a strangely passive creature. A more determined, stronger father might have been able to control his dysfunctional, not to say 'psychotic' family. But David seems paralysed. He follows the advice of others, is cajoled into action by his tough army chief, Joab. His confidence is gone, perhaps, or maybe his mind is on other things; on his poetry, on his prayers.

2 Sam 15.1–12

The death of Absalom is a prime example. This boy, with his film-star good looks, his cold-blooded, calculating violence, his deliberate attempts to belittle his father deserves all that is coming to him.[1] But despite his rebellion, David doesn't want him killed. When a servant brings him the news of the battle, David doesn't care about the victory of his forces – all he cares about is his son. 'Is it well with the young man Absalom?' he keeps asking. And when, finally he hears that it is about as unwell as it's possible to be with Absalom, he screams out one of the most heart-rending cries in all of Scripture:

2 Sam 18.6–19.8

> 'O my son Absalom! My son, my son Absalom! If only I had died instead of you – O Absalom, my son, my son!'

1 Kgs 1.1–4

Broken-hearted fathers, families torn by rivalry and strife, anger, rape, violence and death.

1 Chr 21.18–22.10

1 Kgs 1.25–36

Don't tell me that the Bible's not about real life. There are times when it's so real, it's almost unbearable.

2 Sam 5.9; 1 Kgs 2.10; 1 Chr 11.7

2 Sam 15.6,13

1 While David was supported largely by people from Judah, the south of the country, Absalom's supporters were 'men of Israel' from the ten northern tribes. They were going to regret that.

3.6 Solomon the Wise

Solomon is given great wisdom from God – indeed, his wisdom is legendary. People visit him from throughout the world to hear his thoughts and listen to his learning.

He writes poetry, collects his wise sayings, he writes about biology and zoology. He builds a magnificent new palace in Jerusalem and consolidates all his father's territorial gains.

But it is the temple that really makes his name. His father planned it, but Solomon builds it. Magnificently decorated, it houses the Ark of the Covenant. At the inauguration ceremony a cloud fills the temple; the glory of the Lord.

And yet, and yet...

For all his wisdom, Solomon's reign ends badly. In building of the temple he conscripts labourers from all Israel; but those from the ten northern tribes are treated more harshly than those from the south.

He has seven hundred wives (and three hundred concubines) and many of these wives worship other gods. And they draw Solomon into worshipping those gods as well.

So the 'wise' Solomon ends his life in stupidity – worshipping detestable gods like Chemosh and Molech. He turns away from the God who has given him wisdom and in doing so plunges his kingdom into darkness.

1 Kgs 3.1–15, 10.1–13

1 Kgs 4.29–34

1 Kgs 4.20–27

1 Kgs 8

1 Kgs 12.1–4

Eccl 1.1–11

1 Kgs 11.3–13

Solomon has a reputation: the proverb-writer who is proverbial for his wisdom. But it's not as simple as that.

Yes he's wise. People come from miles to learn from him. Queens sit at his feet. And he builds the temple. Based on the design of Moses's tabernacle, this magnificent building contains the Holy of Holies – the room where the Ark of the Covenant is stored and where only the High Priest is allowed to enter.

But his treatment of the northern tribes is to have catastrophic consequences. Ironically, it's the building of the temple – the building which was supposed to unify Israel – that leads to civil war.[1]

Then there's the end of Solomon's life. He's a compulsive bridegroom, married to women who lure him away to worship Ashtoreth, Milcom, Chemosh and Molech; foreign, useless, evil gods.

Traditionally, Solomon is seen as the writer of Ecclesiastes, that corruscatingly cynical look at the futility of life. Maybe it was his work. Maybe at the end, he could only sum up his wisdom with a weary sigh; 'Meaningless – everything is meaningless.'

1 It's not as if God was that keen on the temple in the first place. When David first broaches the subject of the temple, God says 'Did I ever say to any of their rulers whom I commanded to shepherd my people Israel, Why have you not built me a house of cedar?' (2 Sam 7.7) Not what you'd call a ringing endorsement of the idea.

I'm not worshipping, I've lost a contact lens.

3.7 The Divided Kingdom

When Solomon dies he is succeeded by his son Rehoboam. The ten tribes make clear their resentment of his father's behaviour.. 1 Kgs 11.41–43

Ten Tribes: Your father put a heavy yoke on us, but if you lighten it we will serve you. 1 Kgs 12.1–20

The sensible thing to do would have been to agree, to lighten the duty, to keep the nation together. But Rehoboam rejects the advice of his elders and warns that he will be even tougher than his father.

Rehoboam: Where my father beat you with whips, I will use scorpions.

Bad move. Really, really bad move. The ten northern tribes rebel against Rehoboam, break away into their own kingdom and appoint their own king – a man called Jeroboam. 1 Kgs 12.20

Israel splits into two. The ten northern tribes band together and stay, somewhat confusingly, under the same name: Israel. The southern tribes call themselves Judah (after the biggest tribe). Rehoboam rules Judah, Jeroboam rules Israel.

Immediately, the new northern kingdom of Israel has a problem: the temple is in the south.

If people go to Jerusalem to worship, King Jeroboam worries that they will return to King Rehoboam and the house of David. So he comes up with a plan: as he has a shiny new kingdom, he will have his own temple and, more than that, a shiny new religion. He makes 1 Kgs 12.25–33 two golden calves (not very original) and puts one in Bethel and the other in Dan. Thus, the new kingdom of Israel abandons the faith of its ancestors.

It isn't long before the southern kingdom of Judah follows. King Rehoboam also sets up shrines to false gods. God punishes Rehoboam when the Egyptians attack Jerusalem and cart off many of the golden treasures from the temple. Rehoboam repents and the Lord allows him to carry on as king. But the damage has been done. The seeds have been sown.

1 Kgs 14.21–24

And this is the future pattern. Both kingdoms have leaders who abandon God and worship the false gods of the nations around them.

So God provides an alternative leadership. He empowers a group of people who listen to him and pass his messages on; strange people in some ways, outsiders, truth-speakers, edge-walkers, those who march to the beat of a different drum, who burn with the words of God within them.

The prophets.

Irony. It's not just that the building of the temple causes a split in the kingdom; it also causes a breakaway religion.

The new kingdom proclaims its identity with the worship of new gods. And it is not long before the southern kingdom follows suit.

So, we're left with two disunited, disobedient kingdoms; weak, wandering, led by a succession of evil idiots, picking up on whatever the latest religion is. From now on it's up to the prophets. Because the kings are, frankly, rubbish.

3.8 Elijah

Elijah is a prophet from a small town in the rugged region of Gilead. After announcing a drought as punishment for Israel, he leaves the country and spends some time living in a ravine and being fed by ravens. He ends up in Zarephath in Phoenicia, where, among other miracles, he raises a dead boy to life. He is God's champion.

Israel's king at this time is Ahab, an evil man, who has married Jezebel, an even more evil woman. She is a Phoenician princess and she drives the prophets of the Lord into hiding and imports prophets of Baal from her own land.

Elijah challenges them to a contest. Two bulls are put on two wooden pyres and Elijah challenges the prophets of Baal to summon their god to bring down fire. For hours the Baal prophets cry to their god, with no result.

> Elijah: Shout louder! Maybe he's asleep. Or maybe he's on the toilet!

Desperate, the Baal prophets cut themselves with swords, but it is no use. Nothing happens.

Elijah's turn. He drenches his pyre with water, just to make it a bit more of a challenge. He prays to God and fire from heaven devours the sacrifice, the wood, and even the stones around.

The people all around start chanting 'The Lord is God!' and Elijah commands them to seize the prophets of Baal and kill them.

1 Kgs 17.1–24

1 Kgs 16.29–33

1 Kgs 18.27

1 Kgs 18

Elijah. The über-prophet.

Elijah's name means 'The Lord is God.' He's a figure of almost elemental power, a throwback to Moses and Abraham. Think 'hairy.' Think 'wild.' Think 'deeply unsettling.'

With his rough clothes and wild appearance, Elijah was a living reminder to Israel of the authentic, powerful faith they had abandoned. Nowhere is this demonstrated more clearly than in the raising of the dead boy to life; the first recorded instance in Scripture. Death and rebirth – only God can do that.

His contest with the priests of Baal on the slopes of Mount Carmel is titanic. And also hilarious.[1] Single-handedly he takes on the false prophets and mashes them into the ground.

He proves that there is only one true God. That was his mission, that was what he did.

That was what his name meant.

1 He's so *rude* to them. This is not someone, you feel, who is cut out for the whole inter-faith dialogue sort of thing.

Not only has he defeated the prophets of Baal, he's just invented the barbecue

3.9 Elijah on the Mountain

Jezebel is furious. She swears that she will have Elijah killed, so the prophet flees to hide in the wilderness. Which is where God finds him...

God: What are you doing here, Elijah?

Elijah: I'm the only prophet left. And now they're trying to kill me as well.

God: Go out and stand on the mountain. I'm about to pass by.

Then Elijah sees the Lord. Not in the roaring wind that shakes the mountain, nor in the earthquake which shatters the rocks, not even in the crackling fire which sizzles and spits; no, God is in a gentle whisper which comes after all these things. And when Elijah hears the whisper he covers his face with his cloak and stands at the mouth of the cave.

After that, Elijah goes and calls a young lad called Elisha to be his successor.

Back in Israel, Ahab has illegally taken a vineyard (he had the owner framed and stoned to death) and Elijah confronts him.

Elijah: I have found you to tell you this; the Lord will bring disaster on you and your house. Dogs will feast on your blood.

When Ahab hears this he repents. But soon he is back to his old ways. In the end, he dies in battle alongside Jehoshaphat, the King of Judah.

And the dogs lick the blood out of his chariot.

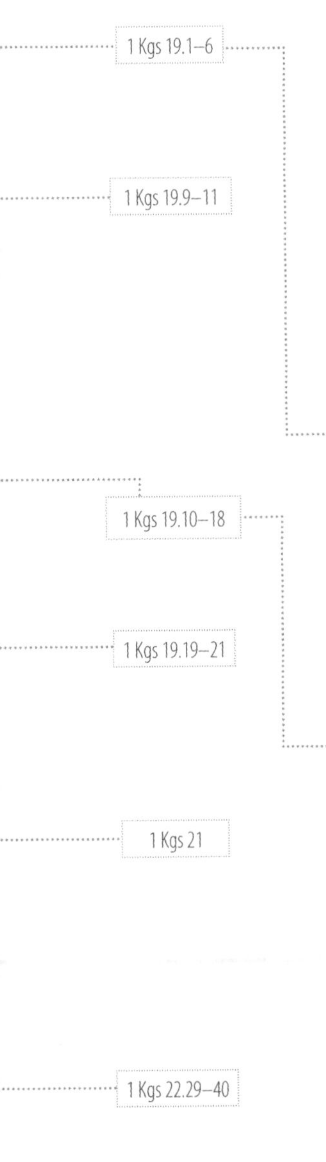

After the heady triumph on Mount Carmel, Elijah crashes back down to earth. Far from being cowed into submission, Jezebel is baying for blood.

What's noticeable about Elijah is how alone he often is. It's not that there aren't other prophets of the Lord around, not that there aren't people who are stubbornly clinging to the old faith. It's just most of them are hiding in caves. (And, to be fair, Elijah spends a lot of time on the run as well.)

So Elijah flees. He sits under a tree and asks to die, but angels bring him cakes.[1] Like Hagar he is saved from death. And strengthened by that food he is in the wilderness for forty days and forty nights. He goes into the wilderness, to Mount Horeb (aka Sinai) – where Moses saw the burning bush and was given the law.

Now who could he possibly meet there?

There is an earthquake, a hurricane and a fire. But it is in something altogether more intimate that God meets Elijah. Elijah's currency was the spectacular – he understood fire and rain and all that. But what God gives him is a soft, gentle whisper. And in that whisper are new instructions for Elijah, a new understanding of who God was, and a new resolve to follow him.

This is Elijah's wilderness encounter. This is where he sees God, and where, perhaps, he finds out that God is not quite what he expected. Far in the future Elijah will stand on a mountain and meet God again. And again, he will be different to what everyone expected.

1 Presumably Angel Cake.

3.10 Elisha and Beyond

Elijah appoints a young man called Elisha to be his successor. Elisha is with his master when a chariot of fire suddenly roars between them and a whirlwind takes Elijah up to heaven.

> Elisha: My father! My father! The chariots and horsemen of Israel!

And with that Elijah is gone. But Elisha has inherited a double-measure of his spirit. Like Elijah, he raises a widow's son from the dead; he heals people from leprosy, he saves people from poisoning. He even captures the entire Syrian army at one point. He is God's agent, travelling around giving messages, performing miracles and challenging disbelief.

And there is a lot of disbelief about. For the history of Israel and Judah in these times is of murder and betrayal and blasphemous disbelief. Jehu takes over Israel, killing Jezebel (she was thrown out of a window although, typically, she had her best make-up on) and cleansing the country from the prophets of Baal.

Meanwhile, in Judah, a woman called Athaliah seizes the throne by killing all her grandchildren and the entire royal family. Well, not quite 'all': one of her grandchildren, Joash, is hidden in the temple. When he is seven, he is brought out of hiding and crowned, and his murderous granny is executed. Joash does some good things (like repairing the temple), but, like so many other kings, he ends up worshipping other gods and is assassinated on his bed at the end.

2 Kgs 11–12

2 Kgs 2.1–18

The fact that Elijah doesn't actually die, but is taken up by God, is always seen by Jews as meaning some day he will return.

However, his work is carried on by his apprentice, Elisha.[1]

2 Kgs 4.8–37, 5.1–19, 4.38–41

Elisha does the same kind of miracles – and more – as his mentor Elijah. He feeds one hundred people using twenty loaves and some grain; he heals people from leprosy; he brings a child back from the dead. But he also acts as a kind of 'statesman prophet', travelling to other lands to appoint people on God's behalf. His travels take him outside the borders of Israel, into Syria.

2 Kgs 6.8–23

His work extends through the reign of six kings and over a period of fifty years. God is broadening the understanding of the Israelites; he is God of the whole world and not just confined to the two nations.

1 His name means 'God is salvation.' He was probably from a fairly prosperous family – when Elijah appointed him he was driving the last of the family's twelve teams of oxen. So they had a lot of oxen, a lot of land, and Elisha was probably the youngest son.

2 Kgs 9.30–37

3.11 The End of Israel

And so it goes on. Kings come, kings go; decades pass and the kingdoms of Israel and Judah go into a long, painful decline, unable to kick their addiction to selfishness, immorality and the worship of fake, foreign gods.

More prophets come to warn them. And one name keeps cropping up: Assyria, the enormous empire to the east, brooding, growing, swelling with power and looking towards Israel and Judah. But the kingdoms do not repent. They do not change their ways.

During the reign of King Menahem of Israel, the Assyrian army sweeps in from the north. The invaders are paid off this time, but it is only temporary and when the Assyrians next invade, again they take away many people to use them as slaves.

(In Judah, King Ahaz decides that imitation is the best form of defence; he copies the Assyrian religion, replacing the fittings in the temple with a copy of the Assyrian altars.)

The end for Israel comes under King Hoshea. He stops paying the Assyrians protection money, they invade and the entire population of Israel are deported to Assyria and replaced with foreign immigrants.

The northern kingdom is over. Only Judah remains. And the Assyrians are looking greedily at them as well.

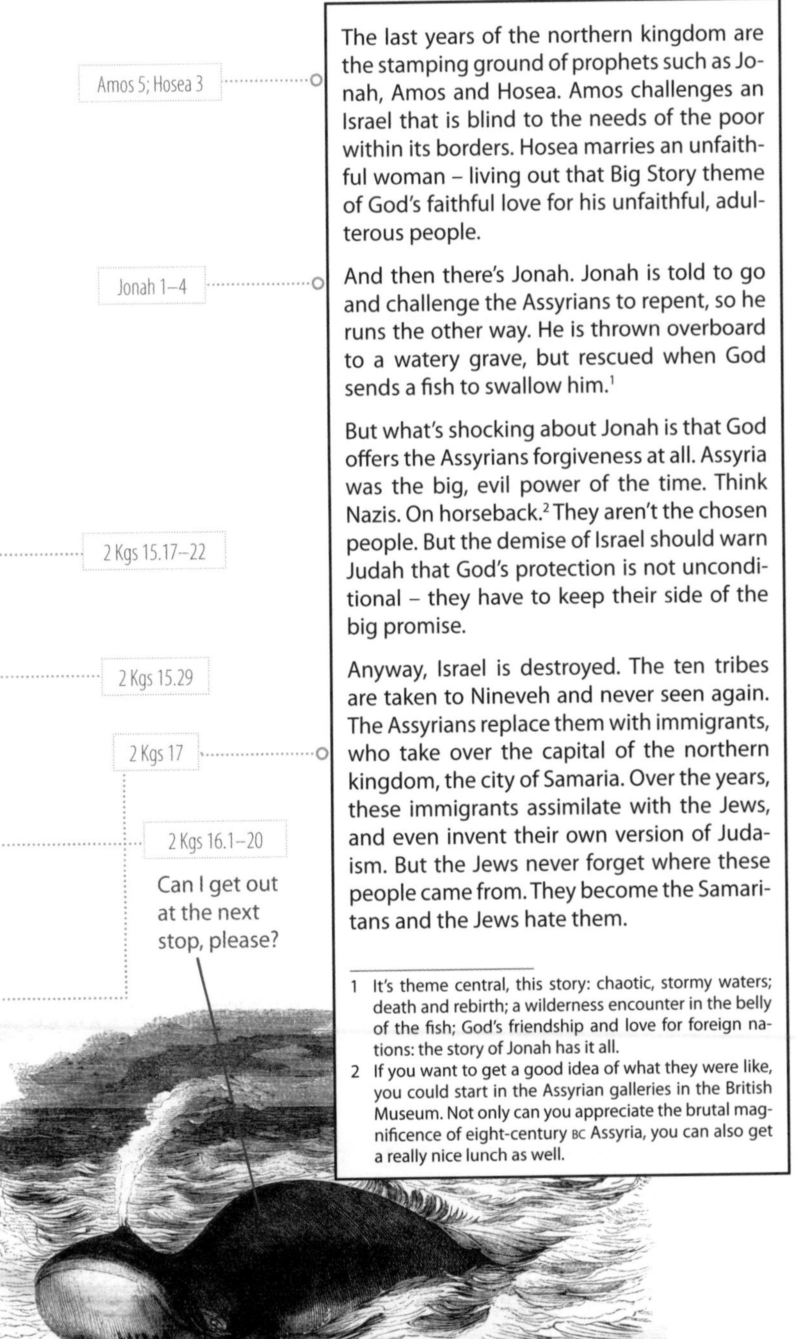

The last years of the northern kingdom are the stamping ground of prophets such as Jonah, Amos and Hosea. Amos challenges an Israel that is blind to the needs of the poor within its borders. Hosea marries an unfaithful woman – living out that Big Story theme of God's faithful love for his unfaithful, adulterous people.

And then there's Jonah. Jonah is told to go and challenge the Assyrians to repent, so he runs the other way. He is thrown overboard to a watery grave, but rescued when God sends a fish to swallow him.[1]

But what's shocking about Jonah is that God offers the Assyrians forgiveness at all. Assyria was the big, evil power of the time. Think Nazis. On horseback.[2] They aren't the chosen people. But the demise of Israel should warn Judah that God's protection is not unconditional – they have to keep their side of the big promise.

Anyway, Israel is destroyed. The ten tribes are taken to Nineveh and never seen again. The Assyrians replace them with immigrants, who take over the capital of the northern kingdom, the city of Samaria. Over the years, these immigrants assimilate with the Jews, and even invent their own version of Judaism. But the Jews never forget where these people came from. They become the Samaritans and the Jews hate them.

1 It's theme central, this story: chaotic, stormy waters; death and rebirth; a wilderness encounter in the belly of the fish; God's friendship and love for foreign nations: the story of Jonah has it all.

2 If you want to get a good idea of what they were like, you could start in the Assyrian galleries in the British Museum. Not only can you appreciate the brutal magnificence of eight-century BC Assyria, you can also get a really nice lunch as well.

3.12 The End of Judah

The northern kingdom is over, but Judah limps on for another 150 years or so.

There are good spells. Like Hezekiah, son of Ahaz the Assyrian-lover, who worships God – unlike his father. Although Assyria attacks during his reign, the Lord intervenes, a plague sweeps through the Assyrian camp and 180,000 men die. So the Assyrians withdraw and, gradually, their empire diminishes. They are never again to threaten Judah.

Hezekiah's reign ends in peace and security. But his son Manasseh is evil. He even puts pagan shrines in the temple of the Lord and he kills followers of the Lord.

Manasseh's son, Amon, is another baddie, but his son Josiah is a reformer. Josiah repairs the temple, during which a copy of the Book of the Law is discovered. Josiah is astonished – he has never heard these words before. He orders everyone to gather in the temple court where he reads to them the Book of the Covenant.

Josiah cleans the country. He reinstitutes Passover – the first proper Passover to be celebrated since the time of the Judges some 500 years earlier. But he dies in battle and his son, Jehoahaz, is another rotten king. It is back to the bad old, wrong-worshipping ways.

These are the days of the great prophets, like Jeremiah and Ezekiel. They warn kings and priests and people of Judah to change, or they will be destroyed. But the people don't listen.

In the end it is the Babylonians who destroy Judah. They are the new superpower. On their first incursion, they take many hostages, including people like Daniel and Ezekiel. They are paid off, but return in the reign of Jehoakim's son, Jehoiachin. The Babylonian emperor, Nebuchadnezzar, orders that all except the very poorest people are taken into exile in Babylon. Jehoiachin's uncle is placed on the throne and renamed Zedekiah.

2 Kgs 24.8–17; Dan 1.1–5; Ezek 1.1–3

2 Kgs 24.18–20

Zedekiah lasts for nine years until he rebels. Once more, Nebuchadnezzar besieges Jerusalem. The suffering is appalling, the once great city of David is reduced to a wreck. The King tries to escape through a hole in the wall, but he is caught. The last thing he sees is his sons, being butchered in front of him. He is blinded, bound and taken to Babylon.

2 Kgs 25.1–7

The temple is stripped; the glory of Solomon is a ruin and the population of Judah are in exile.

Utter, catastrophic defeat.

Jer 32.1–15

Judah ends in a litany of despair and disaster. But there is a flicker of hope. During the Babylonian siege, Jeremiah the prophet bought a field outside Jerusalem, a field, in fact, where Babylonian soldiers were camped. An act of obedient faith which said, 'OK, there are soldiers camped there now, but one day I'm going to see that field.'

The prophets warned Judah of the fate their disobedience would bring. But they also pointed way beyond, to a time when the people would return. They knew that, however disastrous, it was not the end. There would be rescue, redemption from slavery.

God would buy the field.

3.13 Exile

The people of Judah spend many years in exile.

It is a difficult time, when they have to confront the consequences of their own behaviour and the challenges of living in a different culture.

Few people show this as clearly as Daniel, a young prophet who refuses to eat the Babylonian food, preferring to keep to his own dietary laws. When the emperor Nebuchadnezzar has a troubling dream, it is Daniel and not the Babylonian magicians, who is able to interpret it.

Later Nebuchadnezzar sets up a huge gold statue of himself and orders people to worship it. Three young Israelites refuse to do so and are thrown into a huge furnace. Instead of burning up, they are seen walking around, with another figure joining them. When they are brought out, not a hair of their head has been singed.

God is with these people in exile, it seems.

But when will they get home?

What goes around, comes around. Empires rise and empires fall. One night a great feast is held by Belshazzar, the Babylonian emperor. While he is enjoying himself, a mysterious hand appears and writes a mysterious message on the wall. It is all very... mysterious.

Daniel interprets the message: the king's days are numbered; he has been weighed and found wanting. The Persians are coming.

The time in exile is a bewildering time for the Jews. It is a time when the very thing they have always placed their trust in – the land – is taken away from them.

Dan 1.8–21

All the certainties are gone. The temple is destroyed, the people exiled. How could God have allowed this to happen to them? How could they have been so stupid? How are they to worship him, trapped in a strange land thousands of miles from the temple?

Dan 2

And will they ever get home?

Like their heroes, this is the nation's exile period. The time when they lose *everything*.

Dan 3

Faced with the multi-faith society that was Babylon, the exiles do not lose their faith. They change it. Not the substance, but the observation. Without the temple and the sacrificial system to fall back on, Judaism becomes more personal. It isn't that they don't need a temple, but they can operate without one. It isn't that they no longer believe in sacrifice, but they can offer prayer instead.[1]

They have lost homeland, temple, wealth, everything. The northern tribes have gone. They are nobodies now; and that is when they start to realise what was special about them in the first place.

Dan 5

1 And it is at this time, many scholars believe, that the Old Testament Scriptures, all the old stories which have been handed down across the generations, are codified and written down.

3.14 Return

That night the Persian army rides into Babylon and takes over. Their leader, Cyrus the Great, is different. He respects people's religion. He institutes a repatriation policy, allowing the captives in Babylon to return home.

So it is that, under leaders like Nehemiah and Ezra, many of the Israelites end their exile and make the long journey back to Jerusalem, there to begin the long, hard process of rebuilding the city and the temple.

There are many set backs. Neighbouring tribes and people do not want to see Israel restored. So prophets like Haggai and Zechariah encourage people to continue their work.

Not all the Jews return to their homeland, however. Some stay in Babylon. Others go further east, to Susa, capital of the Persian empire.

When the Persian emperor holds a beauty contest to choose a new wife, the winner is a young Jewish girl called Esther. She is instrumental in foiling a plot to kill all the Jews.

Back in Jerusalem, however, things are tough. The Jews rebuild their city and their temple, but it seems such a pale shadow of the glory days under David and Solomon.

The only thing that will change things, they believe, is the Messiah, the long-awaited rescuer, God's anointed one, who will restore Israel to its former glory and usher in an age of peace.

Prophets like Malachi look ahead to his arrival. Mal 3.1–5

But how long will they have to wait?

How long?

Isa 45.1–4; Ezra 1; Jer 25.11, 29.10

Neh 2; Ezra 3.7–13, 7.1–10

Hag 1–2; Zech 1.1–17

Est 2.1–18, 9.24–28

God does, indeed, bring his people back, but the return is not as glorious as they hoped. Reality dawns, cold and hard. They have kept the faith during the exile in Babylon, but keeping the faith back in the rubble of Jerusalem is another matter all together.

During this time, they began to look back on the words of the prophets and see, in Isaiah, Ezekiel and Jeremiah, hints of someone who will restore the glory to Israel. Israel will be great again.

And so the rescue theme becomes personified in the figure of the Messiah, the person who will bring glory back to Israel and rescue them from servitude.[1] They find references to him all over the place in the prophets. He will be a mighty warrior from the house of David. (But read more closely: Isaiah talks about a suffering servant, a scapegoat, a sacrifice to bring redemption, someone who will suffer on behalf of everyone.) Isa 9.6–7, 53.1–12

And so, the Big Story pauses. Israel destroyed. Judah restored. And everyone waiting, holding their breath.

1 Messiah means 'anointed one'.

At which point, we reach the end of the Old Testament.

There will now be an interval of around four hundred years.

During this time Israel will be conquered by the Greek empire and will then rebel and have around one hundred years of independence before being conquered by the Romans; the synagogue system will be developed; the family of Herod will assume the Jewish throne and a range of ice-creams and choc-ices will be served.

A VOICE IN THE WILDERNESS WILL BE HEARD 15 MINUTES BEFORE THE ADVENT OF THE MESSIAH

Act 4
The Messiah

In which we celebrate a virgin birth; welcome the arrival of the long-awaited Messiah; see his life and death and reach a very surprising conclusion.

ACT 4: THE MESSIAH

4.1	The Birth of Jesus
4.2	Baptism and Temptation
4.3	Words and Deeds
4.4	Who is he?
4.5	On the Mountain
4.6	To Jerusalem
4.7	Good Friday
4.8	Great Sunday
4.9	Going Up

CAST

Mary	Mother of Jesus
Joseph	Step-father of Jesus
John the Baptist	Jesus' warm-up act
Jesus	Messiah, miracle-maker, story-teller, Saviour
Peter	A disciple
John	Another disciple
Judas	A traitor
Mary **Martha** **Lazarus**	Friends of Jesus, at least one of whom is not at all well
Pilate	Roman Governor

Various angels, followers, disciples, soldiers, pharisees, etc.

4.1 The Birth of Jesus

It is the reign of Herod the Great. Israel is now 'Palestine', a province in the Roman empire. And the Messiah has been a long time coming.

In Jerusalem, a priest called Zechariah is in the temple, when an angel appears to tell him that his wife, Elizabeth, is going to have a baby. (Since she is old, he finds this hard to believe, so the angel strikes him dumb.) In the fullness of time, Elizabeth gives birth to a boy. She and Zechariah call the boy John. Lk 1.1–23

Elizabeth's cousin is a young girl called Mary. She is engaged to a carpenter called Joseph, and the Angel of the Lord appears to tell her that she, too, will have a baby, even though she is a virgin. The father is God and the child is to be called Jesus. Lk 1.26–56

Faced with Mary's pregnancy, Joseph decides to divorce her quietly, as he does not want to shame the girl. Then an angel appears to him in a dream and reveals to him the truth. Mt 1.18–25

Mary and Joseph travel to Bethlehem for a Roman census. Unable to find a room in an inn, the couple shelter in a cave and there Mary gives birth to a boy called Jesus. Shepherds come to worship the child, alerted to the birth by angels. Lk 2.1–7 Lk 2.8–20

Wise men from the east come to Palestine, looking for a new prince, following a star. It's news to King Herod, who instructs them to Mt 2.1–12

I think I've just invented the Christmas card

return when they find the baby. (He plans to get rid of this imposter.)

They discover Jesus in a house in Bethlehem and give him gifts. But they do not return to Herod and when the king realises, he rages, white-hot, star-bright. He sends troops into Mt 2.16–18
Bethlehem with orders to kill all boys under the age of two. The streets of Bethlehem are filled with blood; the houses with the sound of weeping.

But Mary and Joseph are not there. The family Mt 2.13–15
escape to Egypt where they remain until Herod dies. Then, safe, they return to Palestine. Mt 2.19–23

Jesus grows up in the small community of Lk 2.39–40
Nazareth. He follows in his father's footsteps, Mk 6.3
becoming a builder.

Two births. The first a familiar Big Story theme: the baby born to elderly parents who have given up hope. They're *always* special, those babies. He'll be the messenger. The second, even more miraculous: a girl, around fourteen years old, not yet married, never had sex, and now carrying a child. He'll be the Messiah.

And more meaningful names. John, which means 'the Lord is gracious', is to bring news of that grace. And Jesus – Joshua in Hebrew – meaning 'He whose salvation is the Lord.' An ordinary name, a common name, like calling the Messiah Joe or Dave. And he takes on an ordinary job in a nondescript little town.[1]

But *Joshua*. Dwell on that for a moment. That's got some weight to it, that name. The first Joshua took the Israelites into the Promised Land; where will this Joshua take us?

1 Although he is usually described as a 'carpenter', the Greek word is *tekton*, which really means 'builder' – someone used to working in wood, stone, or metal.

4.2 Baptism and Temptation

Fast forward twenty years or so. In the desert, a voice rings out. A wild man among the rocks; a ragged preacher, a second Elijah. His name is John and people call him 'the baptist' because that's what he does: he washes people in water to make them clean – inside and out.

This is Jesus' cousin – the John born to Elizabeth and Zechariah. He calls people to repent. The people ask if he is the Messiah, but John denies this. He is just preparing the way for someone else.

In time, Jesus comes to his cousin to be baptised, but John refuses. He sees that Jesus has no need to repent. But Jesus insists.

As the river water rinses over him, a voice booms across the valley and a dove descends. And the people looking on feel like they have been through thunder.

After his baptism, Jesus goes up into the wilderness, where he spends forty days without food. The Devil comes to him with prizes, promises, temptations to lure him astray. He offers Jesus food; he promises him power; he tempts him to prove himself once and for all. Jesus refuses these snares, countering with quotations from Scripture.

Thwarted, the devil retreats and angels come to look after the son of God.

2 Kgs 1.8

Isa 40.3; Mal 3.1; Mt 3.1–12, 17.9–13; Mk 1.4–8; Jn 1.19–28

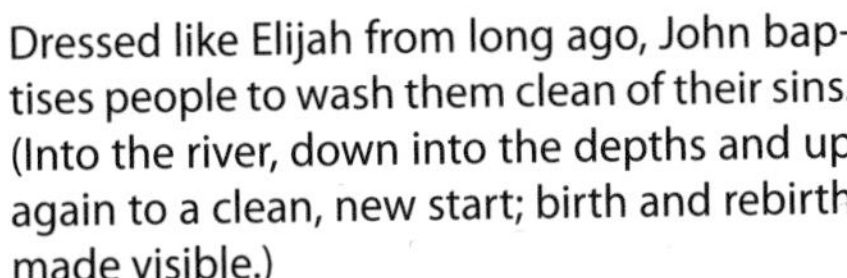

Dressed like Elijah from long ago, John baptises people to wash them clean of their sins. (Into the river, down into the depths and up again to a clean, new start; birth and rebirth made visible.)

Then Jesus comes along. The sinless Son of God saying sorry for sin? Doesn't work, somehow, and John knows it. But Jesus plays by the rules. This is what his Father wants him to do and his Father demands obedience.

Jn 1.19–23

So this is the way that Jesus' work has to start. But then it's out into the desert. No food. Forty days. It's like all the themes of the Big Story are coalescing in this man's life; you can feel them, massing together, building up.

Mt 3.13–17; Mk 1.9–11; Lk 3.21–22

Mt 4.1–11; Mk 1.12–13; Lk 4.1–13

In the desert Jesus confronts demons. Well, the main demon, to be precise. Yes it's the serpent back again, only without the snakeskin costume. It's Adam and Eve time, and this time what tasty fruit has Satan got to dangle before his victim's eyes?

He offers Jesus three tempting morsels: some food to eat (well, it worked the first time); power (the opportunity to rule the world) and prestige (the chance to show who he really was).

Oh, this is clever, this is *subtle*. He's using one of the most dangerous lures: the urge to do the expected. He's tempting Jesus to be the kind of Messiah that everyone expects – powerful, princely, prestigious. But Jesus does the unexpected. He opts for discipline, servanthood, suffering.

He's the unexpected Messiah. The surprising Christ. The king of the upside-down kingdom. And what worked with Adam and Eve has failed this time around.

I'm thinking of launching my own range of swimwear.

4.3 Words and Deeds

There are miracles: dishwater made into wedding wine, demons destroyed, people healed, restored, made whole.

And there are words. In the synagogues and on the hillsides, Jesus teaches the crowds. He talks to the poor, the hungry, the spiritually malnourished, the lonely and unloved. He teaches people how to pray. He urges them to put their faith in God and not in man. He boils down the law and the prophets to a handful of words.

Jesus: Love the Lord your God. And love your neighbour as yourself.

On Galilee, some fishermen take him out so that he can speak to the crowds. When he fills their nets to overflowing with fish, these simple fishermen join Jesus and fish for followers.

Fishermen! For a holy man he has unholy friends – tax-collectors and prostitutes, the discarded, the impure, the outcasts. And he's always partying; always eating, drinking, laughing and upsetting people.

His family worry that he has gone mad. Even his cousin questions. But John is in jail, having criticised the king – one of old Herod's sons – for his scandalous love life. There, John is executed; his head delivered on a platter, the result of a stupid, drunken vow. When Jesus hears this, he goes to a desolate place to be on his own. But the crowds follow him, desperate for healing, hungry for hope.

He's a miracle-worker this Jesus, in the tradition of Elijah and Elisha. Only bigger. Elijah prayed and a pot of oil went on for years. But that only fed three people. Jesus lifts a hand and the nets are overflowing and hundreds, even thousands, are fed.

Mt 4.24, 8.16, 15.30; Mk 1.34; Lk 4.40; Jn 2.1–11

It's not the miracles that are the problem. He's a holy man – miracles come with the territory. And the teaching – although its contents might annoy and upset the religious leaders – well, that's what holy men do as well.

Mt 13.54; Mk 6.2; Lk 4.16–30

Mt 5.1–12, 6.5–13, 6.25–34; Lk 12.22–31

No, it's the friendships which are the problem. It's the company he keeps. The kingdom he proclaims is widening out, including the most unlikely folk. This Jesus chooses the unchosen; he selects the unselectable.

Mt 7.12, 22.34–40

Fishermen! What kind of followers are they? Rough, ready, uncultured, uneducated and generally smelling of, well, fish.

Mt 4.18–22; Mk 1.16–20; Lk 5.1–11

And it gets worse. He recruits hated tax-collectors – who collude with the Romans in bribery and extortion. He mixes with prostitutes and lepers – all those who have no place, it is generally agreed, in the kingdom of heaven.

Mk 2.15–17

And he spends far too much time drinking, eating and celebrating. He lingers with them, explains things to them, shares deep truths with them.

Mk 3.21

What kind of holy man befriends such unholy people? And what, they wonder, has he got to be so happy about?

Mk 6.14–29; Mt 14.1–12; Lk 9.7–9

Actually, I'm allergic to fish.

Now all that we need is the invention of the chip.

4.4 Who is He?

The question on the lips of both friend and foe is 'Who is this man?'

Lepers are healed, demons are cast out, lessons are learned. Thousands of people are fed with a few flat loaves and a couple of fish. He quietens storms – storms on the lakes and storms in the hearts of troubled souls. He attacks hypocrisy; he is wonder-worker, healer, teacher, life-changer, story-teller.

Ah yes, the stories...

They cling to the mind like limpets; they make the listeners laugh, think, react. They are outrageous, unlikely, impressive, simple in structure but rich in meaning. There are farmers and fools; princes and peasants; wedding guests and widows; travellers, tenants, shepherds and sons. All manner of people in all kinds of tales.

More followers are called; twelve men to be his core team but others – 72 of them – to go out and spread the good news. And women follow him and support him.

But who is he? Where does he get all this stuff from?

Peter sees. Peter knows.

Peter: You are the Messiah. The Son of God.

The truth, then. But no-one, apparently, is to be told.

Mt 16.13–20;
Mk 8.27–30;
Lk 9.18–27

Mt 14.13–21; Mk 6.30–44; Lk 9.10–17; Jn 6.1–14

Mt 14.22–33; Mk 6.45–52; Jn 6.15–21

Mt 11.2–6

Lk 10.1–12

You expect the author of the Big Story to be good at story-telling, but even so...

Has there ever been a better story-teller? 'The kingdom of God is like this...' they often begin. And that's what they are about; pictures of God's realm; they show what being a citizen of that kingdom is like. They draw on the world around him, but in God's kingdom things happen upside-down. Enemies show love; failures are forgiven; renegade sons are welcomed home with a party. His stories come from the world around him, but they are gateways to another world entirely.

And the kingdom was not just in the stories but invading real life as well. People came to see Jesus in action – to witness (or experience themselves) the healings and the casting out of demons. They came to look, and they stayed to listen.

'Go back,' he told them, 'and tell your own stories. Say what you see – the blind can see, the lame can run, the lepers are clean, the deaf can hear, the dead come back to life.' The revolution has started.

What he did showed who he was. What he said showed what he wanted of us. And who he is – well, like in all the best stories the truth is being revealed bit by bit. Here, Peter jumps ahead of the plot; skips to the end. He's the Christ, the Messiah, the Rescuer.[1] He's the hero of the Big Story.

But Jesus, like all the best story tellers, doesn't want the ending revealed quite yet. These things have to be told properly.

1 More names. 'Christ' is the Greek version of the Hebrew word 'Messiah'. Nowadays we tend to say 'Jesus Christ' as though 'Christ' was his surname. But it really means 'Jesus the Messiah'.

4.5 On the Mountain

Jesus goes up a mountain with Peter, John and James. His followers start to doze, but they are woken by a bright light. As they look at Jesus, they see that his face has changed and his clothing is dazzlingly white.

As they look on, they see Jesus talking with two other figures, and somehow the disciples just know that these are Moses and Elijah. And they talk with Jesus about what he has yet to do. A cloud covers the mountain and God's voice is heard.

God: This is my Son, the chosen one. Listen to him!

And when the voice fades away there is Jesus alone. And there is only silence.

Who is this man? Friend of Moses and Elijah. And, like Elijah, able to raise the dead. But Elijah only did this once; Jesus does it loads. A widow's son in Nain, the daughter of a local official. And in Bethany he brings back his friend Lazarus to life. But unlike Elijah, Jesus does this in his own power.

Bethany is only a little way Jerusalem. Some of those who are watching go and report these things to the Pharisees. And the day when Lazarus was brought back to life, is the day they started plotting to put Jesus to death.

Mt 17.1–13; Mk 9.2–13; Lk 9.28–36

Hello, we're up a mountain again. And we're with two of the people who got to see God in all his glory – or a bit of him anyway – Moses and Elijah.

And who are they meeting with this time? It's Jesus himself.

God on the mountain-top, a face irradiated by holiness. Themes from elsewhere in the Big Story are bubbling and boiling and thickening around this man Jesus.

He's like Moses in that he's laying down a new law for people to follow; he's like Elijah in that he's showing them who God is. But more than both of these, greater than either.

Mt 9.18–26, 11.5; Mk 5.35–43; Lk 7.11–17; Jn 11.1–44

And all around him the pattern of death and rebirth plays. It's not just the real resurrections – the in-your-face, up-and-walking corpses – though these are amazing enough. No, it's all the 'little' resurrections. Tax collectors climb a tree and come down a different person. Women whose bleeding bodies have barred them from holiness get to touch God, and suddenly they are clean and whole as they have never been in their life. Lepers – those poor souls caught in living death – are cured. People meet him and something dies and something is reborn.

Jn 3.1–15

But for all his followers some kind of death is necessary. He tells one follower that no one gets to see the kingdom unless they have been reborn, unless they believe in him and want to start again.

Death and rebirth. For everyone.

4.6 To Jerusalem

After three years of working in Galilee and throughout Judea, Jesus decides to go up to Jerusalem again.

His disciples are appalled, arguing that he will be in peril. But he insists. He is walking a path, working to a plan, pushing his way through a very narrow door. But the road smells of danger and death.

And still the crowds gather to see him. Blind men are healed. In Jericho, a tax-collector climbs a tree to get a better view and his life is changed. Wherever he goes, Jesus helps people to see more clearly.

Mt 9.27–31
Mk 8.22–26
Jn 9.1–17

As he draws near to Jerusalem he cries over it. He weeps over the holy city, for the unholy way it has always treated its holy men. But he enters the city in triumph, through the gates, the people cheering and waving palm leaves and throwing their cloaks on the road for his donkey to walk on. (The leaders look on, worried where this will lead.)

Mt 21.1–11;
Mk 11.1–11
Lk 19.28–44
Jn 12.12–19

It is the beginning of the last week of his life.

On Monday he causes trouble. In the temple he drives out the money-lenders, who sell blessings and short-change the pilgrims. (The leaders begin to plan his arrest and death.)

Mt 21.12–17
Mk 11.15–19
Lk 19.45–46
Jn 2.13–22

The next evening he sits on the Mount of Olives, overlooking the city and talks about what will happen in the end, about the times at the end of time. He talks of the temple being torn down, he will return and the whole world will see, but not even he knows when that will be, exactly. (That night, his enemies recruit Judas, offering him thirty pieces of silver to sell Jesus to them.)

Mt 24; Mk 13; Lk 21.5–38

Lk 22.3–6

On the Thursday, Jesus and his followers share their final meal. During the meal he – their leader – takes off his clothes and washes their feet like a lowly servant. He breaks bread and wine with them, and orders them to recall him whenever they do the same.

After supper they go down into the Garden of Gethsemane to pray. There, Jesus prays in anguish, while his disciples struggle to keep their eyes open. Suddenly a great crowd of men appear, with clubs and swords and led by Judas. He kisses his former leader. And Jesus is arrested.

Mt 26.36–56; Mk 14.32–50; Lk 22.39–53; Jn 18.1–14

The past is thick around Jesus; with every step he kicks up the dust of history. Look at the echoes here. He enters Jerusalem in triumph; the city of his ancestor David, the shepherd-king. He throws cheats out of the temple, challenging fake religion like the prophets did.

Ex 12

Then, he brings the rescue story right up to date. Passover celebrated God's rescue of his people from slavery; this new meal will celebrate another rescue – a greater rescue – from a darker slavery.

Ex 24.8; Mk 14.24; Isa 53.4–6; 1 Cor 11.23–26

And with the new Passover a new promise of friendship with God. The promises in the past were marked by sacrifices, and this will be the same. Only different, because it will be Jesus, the suffering servant seen by Isaiah, who will sacrifice himself to bring humanity and God back together.

So, we see Jesus surfing history here; wearing the clothes of the old stories; bringing everything to one, great conclusion.

4.7 Good Friday

Mt 26.57–75
Mk 14.53–72
Lk 22.54–71
Jn 18.12–27

Late on Thursday night Jesus is taken to the High Priest, found guilty of blasphemy and imprisoned. Outside, in the courtyard, Peter is spotted, but denies knowing Jesus and flees. The rest of his followers have dissolved into the darkness.

Mt 27.11–26
Mk 15.1–15;
Lk 23.1–25;
Jn 18.28–40

There are hurried, confused trials. He faces, Herod, Pilate the Roman Governor and the religious high council. Through all his trials, Jesus hardly says a word.

Mt 27.3–10;
Acts 1.17–19

(Meanwhile Judas, seeing Jesus is condemned, repents of what he has done. He flings the blood money back at the Jewish leaders and goes and hangs himself.)

Pilate tries to let Jesus go, but the crowd have been turned. Jesus is beaten, then taken to a hill just outside the city. At nine in the morning he is nailed to a cross.

Mt 27.27–5
Mk 15.16–4
Lk 23.26–4
Jn 19.17–3

Over him hangs a sign 'This is Jesus – King of the Jews' and on his head the soldiers have rammed a cruel, mocking crown of thorns. On either side of him are two thieves. The people passing by shout at him to save himself, if he can. One of the thieves even mocks him, but the other sees through the pain to who Jesus is. Jesus promises him a place in paradise.

Jn 19.25–27

His followers and family gaze on from a distance in hopeless despair. Jesus asks John to look after Mary, his mother.

At midday the skies turn dark.

At three in the afternoon, Jesus gives a last, pained, tortured cry. It is finished. He is dead. Mt 27.45–50 Mk 15.33–37

There are reports that the huge curtain in the temple has been torn in two. The earth shakes. People see tombs cracked open and ghosts walking the street. The weirdness is everywhere. Mt 27.51–54; Mk 15.38–39; Lk 23.44–45

His body is taken down. A rich follower called Joseph of Arimathea has a tomb nearby, and he takes charge of the body. Jesus' corpse is carried the short distance to a nearby cave. It is wrapped in a linen shroud and the huge stone is rolled across the doorway. Mt 27.57–61; Mk 15,42–47; Lk 23.50–56; Jn 19.38–42

Later, the Jews post a guard to make sure nothing could happen to the body. Mt 27.62–66

Fat chance.

Now we're into the deepest, darkest themes. We're talking sacrifice; as old as Cain and Abel. We're talking the Son's death, on the hill where Abraham stood, knife raised, many centuries before. We're talking about all those animals sacrificed under the old law to restore the relationship between God and man. But this... this is bigger than all of them. This is the ultimate sacrifice; the once-for-all.

But understanding that comes later. For now, all they know is that something big is happening. This is the pivotal moment. This is the pause before the punchline, the still point where everything in the story hangs in the balance. 3 p.m. Friday, 3 April, 33AD.[1]

Creation cries out. The temple curtain is torn; now anyone can walk into the Holy of Holies, where God is supposed to dwell. The old certainties are crumbling; the tombs are cracking open and the dead are walking again. Death, it appears, is in retreat.

At this point, at this moment, the future is dark. And no-one knows if the Big Story is going to have a happy ending or not.

1 Well, that's what I reckon. Although some argue for Friday 7 April 30AD. Sir Isaac Newton, apparently, favoured 34AD. But then he had been hit on the head by a very large apple.

4.8 Great Sunday

On Sunday morning, Mary Magdalene and some other women go to the tomb to anoint the body. But the tomb is empty. The huge stone has been rolled back and an angel is sitting on it. The guards lie around, stunned and senseless with fear.

Angel: Don't be afraid. You're looking for Jesus, but he's not here. He's risen.

The women rush back to tell the others. But Mary Magdalene stands, weeping. Turning around, she sees the gardener.

Mary: Please, where have you taken him? Tell me where he is and I'll look after the body.

The gardener turns and says her name and suddenly all the dead flowers in Mary's life blossom again. It is not the gardener but God; Jesus, risen from the dead. He warns her not to touch him, but to go and tell the others.

That day loads of people see him. The women see him in the garden. Two men meet him as they trudge towards Emmaus. He slips through a locked door to meet the disciples.

For the next month or so he keeps appearing. He confronts Thomas (who missed the first showing). His brother James sees him. He appears to more than five hundred of his followers. The disciples meet him back in Galilee. He gives them a miraculous catch of fish then cooks them a barbecue. And Peter, who hid during the trial, is loved and restored and forgiven.

Mt 28.1–10; Mk 16.1–8; Lk 24.1–12; Jn 20.1–10

New life. Something out of nothing. Shoots that winter looked to have killed, pushing up through the spring soil.

Mary mistakes him for the gardener, taking us right back to the beginning, when God would wander round Eden. And now this garden is bursting with hope, buzzing with new life. He's back. And with him comes the chance to go back to the garden.[1]

Jn 20.11–18

Indeed, there's something wonderfully earthy about Jesus' post-resurrection appearances. They are the opposite of ghostly. I mean, all right, he walks through doors, which haven't actually been opened, but he offers Thomas the chance to feel his wounds. Actually *feel* them.

And then, on the beach, in Galilee, when the disciples have gone back to the old job for a bit and are out fishing on the lake, once again he gives them masses of fish, taking them back to the miracle that occurred when first they were invited to join the Big Story.

Lk 24.13–35

But then he grills some and cooks a fish barbecue. Now show me the ghost that does that.

1 Cor 15.3–7

Mt 28.16–20; Lk 24.36–49; Jn 20.19–21.25

It's the *number* of appearances as well. He doesn't just appear to a select few, but to masses. He appears to his family, to women, to two troubled souls walking along the road out of Jerusalem and wondering where it all went wrong. Let's face it. He's back. Death and rebirth.

God's gardening again.

1 Have you noticed how often people envisage the perfect place as a garden on a summer's day? Paradise. Which comes from, I believe, the old Persian word for 'garden'.

4.9 Going Up

They are back in Jerusalem, and Jesus comes to them one final time. He tells them that he will be sending someone else, another Companion to be with his followers forever. This Being will enable them to take the good news to the ends of the earth.

Then, as they look, he is lifted up into the sky, and disappears into a cloud. There are two figures there.

> Angels: Why do you look up into heaven? Jesus who was taken up there will return in the same way.

And with that the disciples leave the Mount of Olives and return to Jerusalem, to the Upper Room which, since his resurrection, is the unofficial headquarters of this new movement.

Sometimes the angels seem not to understand humans. I mean, what a question to ask; 'Why do you look up into heaven?'

'Because he's just gone up there, that's why. Unlike you, we don't see that many people fly upwards. So, we're trying to see where he went. You got a problem with that?'

Acts 1.1–12

Jesus has gone up and one day, who knows when – he'll be coming back down again. This act of the Big Story ends with Jesus returning to his original home; back to heaven.

But he won't be leaving for good. He'll be coming back for the finalé. The return of Jesus. The second coming. No one knows when it's going to happen or what exactly is going to happen. The Bible gives clues, paints pictures, but only God knows the date and time.[1]

So the disciples (probably now with bad cricks in their necks) return to the room to wait for the next arrival.

They started out as a bunch of nobodies; a rag-tag band of followers, tax-collectors, fishermen, political agitators, all kinds of people caught in the same net. And now they have been caught up in events that have surprised them all.

Now they're about to be reborn. To be transformed.

But into what?

Mk 13.32

1 Even Jesus doesn't know the precise details.

Act 5
The Church

In which we see a ragged bunch of Jesus' followers turn into a world-changing movement; meet a persecutor turned follower called Saul; encounter persecution and false teaching; and finally see how the whole thing is going to end.

ACT 5: THE CHURCH

5.1	Pentecost
5.2	Saul's Conversion
5.3	The Gentile Church
5.4	The Council
5.5	Paul's Journeys
5.6	The Fall of the Temple
5.7	New Heaven, New Earth

CAST

Peter	Apostle, church leader
John	Apostle, old bloke, visionary
Stephen	Martyr
Saul/Paul	Persecutor of the church turned champion of Christ
Barnabas	An encouraging bloke
James	Brother of Jesus and first leader of the Jerusalem church
Timothy	Church leader
Mark	Writer and evangelist
Luke	Writer and travelling companion of Paul
Matthew	Apostle and writer

Various Christians, angels, Romans, Jews, Gentiles, Proconsuls, Emperors, soldiers, sailors, etc...

5.1 Pentecost

The disciples cast lots to decide who should replace Judas. Matthias takes his place.

It is Pentecost, some fifty days after the death and resurrection of Jesus. The followers are gathered together when there is a sound like a mighty rushing wind which fills the entire house. Tongues of fire appear, flickering above their head and suddenly they begin to speak in all kinds of languages. All the pilgrims to the festival – Jews from throughout the Mediterranean – can hear these rough Galileans speaking their language.

Peter preaches the good news and that day around three thousand people are baptised and join the followers.

These early followers gather together most days to pray, study the Scriptures and share bread together. Everybody shares what they have.

Many signs and wonders are done through the apostles. Peter and John heal a lame beggar and are hauled before the council, who cannot comprehend how these simple fishermen have a boldness, a power, an other-worldliness that sets them apart.

So the followers continue to increase in number. So much so that the apostles appoint seven deacons to oversee practical matters, such as the care of widows and orphans.

Acts 1.14–26

They were not drunk. That's what some people claimed – those who heard the Galileans talking in all kinds of languages; they thought they were drunk. But as Peter said, 'It's too early in the morning.' Not drunkenness then, but high spirits. Or Holy Spirit, to be exact.

Acts 2

Jesus has gone, but he has sent another to be with his followers. The Holy Spirit is the third part of the triangle that is God. The Spirit is his life-giving power – the bit of God that dwells inside us, spurring us on, bringing us comfort, telling us what to do, making us more like Christ.

Rewind to Pentecost. The Holy Spirit appears like 'tongues' of fire on their heads and sets the disciples ablaze. It's Babel reversed. At Babel humans grasped up to be like God; here God has already come down to be one of them. Now all the nations can understand. Now language is no longer a barrier.

Acts 2.42–47, 4.32–37

Acts 3.1–4.22

The Holy Spirit sends them out to talk about all they have seen and heard, to spread the good news. And the Spirit empowers them to live right. Everything is shared, the poor are provided for, the Scriptures are scoured, prayers are prayed, bread is broken, wine is drunk, the kingdom has secured a bridgehead on earth and it's invading fast. So fast that they have to appoint more leaders; administrators to organise the feeding of the poor. But such is the overwhelming power of the Holy Spirit that these seven start preaching and performing miracles themselves.

Acts 6.1–7

No respecter of structures, God.

Hates organisation charts, probably.

5.2 Saul's Conversion

As the numbers increase, and the signs and wonders continue, the temperature rises. Things are coming to boiling point. Peter and John are beaten. One of the deacons, a man named Stephen (who, also, has been performing miracles) is accused of blasphemy. After making a courageous and outspoken defence of his faith, he is taken outside the city and stoned.

Acts 6.8–7.60

(And those who stone him, take off their coats and leave them in the care of a zealous young Pharisee called Saul.)

The death of Stephen launches a wave of persecution on the young church. The followers scatter – heading mainly north, to Samaria and beyond.

Acts 8.1–25

But Saul the Pharisee follows them. Not just a coat-holder, then, but a persecutor, an enforcer, given the task of reducing this new heresy to a pile of rubble.

He is approaching Damascus when, suddenly, a burst of light blinds him, knocks him to the ground. And he hears the voice of Jesus, calling him to stop his opposition.

Blind, helpless, his whole world turned upside down, Saul's colleagues lead him into the city. For three days he sits in the dark, neither eating nor drinking. Then a follower called Ananias is sent to Saul (bravely overcoming his fear, such was Saul's reputation). Ananias prays for him. Suddenly Saul can see again. He gets up, is baptised and starts eating.

Acts 9.1–19; Gal 1.11–17

Saul is a changed man. He goes straight into the synagogues and starts telling everyone about Jesus. Eventually the Jews plot to kill this turncoat, and he has to be spirited out of Damascus at night, in a laundry basket.

When Saul first meets the disciples in Jerusalem, they are wary of him, but a follower called Barnabas supports his cause. Typically, Paul goes to the synagogues and gets into arguments, so in the end he is packed off to Caesarea and thence to his home city of Tarsus. And he stays there for around ten years.

Meanwhile, the good news is spreading. As Gentiles as well as Jews, turn to Christ, Peter hears from God: no person is common or unclean before God. Gentiles should also be baptised in the name of Christ.

(But back at Jerusalem, there are Jewish followers – the circumcision party – who believe that all followers of Jesus should follow Jewish law as well. And they are not convinced.)

The martyrdom of Stephen backfires on the religious leaders. Like throwing water on a chip pan fire, all it does is spread the blaze. And it spreads so fast and so furiously that even one of the chief fire-fighters get caught in the conflagration.

Saul is knocked sideways by an encounter with the risen Christ. He is gamekeeper turned poacher; the royalist becomes the rebel.[1] The old Saul is dead and a new Paul is on its way.

1 And where does this happen? On the road through the desert, of course.

5.3 The Gentile Church

Years pass. At Antioch a new church flickers into being, made up of Gentiles. Barnabas is sent to oversee it and he fetches Saul from Tarsus. (And the people in Antioch are the first to call these followers 'Christians'.)

Things are tough in Jerusalem. Herod is persecuting the church. He beheads James, the brother of John and Peter is arrested (although he is rescued by an angel).

There is a famine as well. Saul and Barnabas take aid to Jerusalem from the Syrian church. While there, Saul explains that he has been given the task of taking the gospel to the Gentiles.

So it is that, a few weeks later, he sets off, with Barnabas and a young Jewish Christian called John Mark, on a missionary journey into Gentile territory. They start in Cyprus (where they defeat a magician called Elymas). John, for some reason, returns to Jerusalem, but Saul and Barnabas head up to Antioch in Pisidia. (From this point on, Saul becomes known by his Greek name – Paul.)

The opposition they face is immense. There are beatings and stonings and hatred and enmity. But Paul is determined that Gentiles should be saved and in Lystra, Derbe and Iconium, he sets up churches and appoints leaders.

Acts 11.19–26

The church has broken the boundaries. It has spread beyond Palestine, into Syria.

In Antioch, Gentiles join the followers. In the early years there are several names for the church. Those who followed Jesus were called Nazirites, or Followers of the Way.[1] But at Antioch they find the name that has stuck ever since: Christians.[2]

Acts 9.2, 19.9, 23

Acts 12.1–19

It is probably ten years now since Saul fell off his horse. He has been in various places: Arabia, Damascus, mainly Tarsus. He has been learning how to talk about Christ, reading Scripture, thinking about things.

Acts 11.27–30; Gal 2.1–10

Now he is ready to go. The church has spread north, but it hasn't been a conscious decision; nobody sat down and planned it that way. With Paul it's different. Paul looks at the world he knows and wonders why everyone hasn't heard about Christ. Paul looks at roads and cities and plans to go and tell them.

Acts 13.1–14

So he heads through Cyprus and then up into the heart of Galatia, for the first time deliberately going to the Gentiles and taking them the message of Jesus.

And back in Jerusalem alarm bells start ringing...

1 They may also have been called the *Eboni*, which means 'The Poor'. Obviously they hadn't consulted any marketing men. I mean, who wants to voluntarily join the poor?

2 The nickname was probably given to them by non-believing Gentiles in the city. It means 'Christ followers,' or 'those of the household of Christ'. Although it would have started as a derisive term, actually it was prescient. These people understood that the new movement was more than a variant of Judaism. It was more than an extension of the Jewish household. It was a whole new building.

5.4 The Council

Paul might be convinced about the Gentiles: others are not so sure.

Back in Antioch, the circumcision party hear about Paul's missionary work and they try to force the Gentile Christians to follow the Jewish law. Even Peter slips back into his old ways.

Paul is forced to confront this head on. He writes to the Galatian churches he has just founded and encourages them to stick fast to what he has taught them.

It comes to a head in a council meeting in Jerusalem. Peter takes up the cause of the Gentiles. His view is echoed by James, the brother of Jesus, and leader of the church in Jerusalem. (A devout man, he is praised by both Jew and Christian for his law-abiding behaviour.) After the assembly hears from Paul and Barnabas about all that has been happening on their travels, James declares that Gentile Christians should not have to be circumcised. They are Christians and not Jews.

Triumphant, Paul and Barnabas return to Antioch, with some other brothers sent by the church in Jerusalem. Paul suggests another trip to Barnabas, but they argue: Barnabas wants to take John Mark, Paul feels he is unreliable. In the end Barnabas goes off to Cyprus with John Mark, while Paul takes Silas.

They are never to travel together again.

Acts 15.1–2; Gal 2.11–21

Are we Jewish or not? This was the question that the church grappled with in its early years. At first, of course, like their founder, they were all Jews (even though some of those Jews came from Greek cities). But then things started to overflow. Gentiles heard the great news about Jesus and they wanted to be a part of the story.

Paul had been doing some hard thinking and he'd begun to see that it wasn't about the law, it was about faith. Things like circumcision and sacrifice had been superseded by Jesus;[1] Jesus' life, death and resurrection had broken down the barriers between humanity and God. Our sinfulness meant that we should die; but Jesus sacrificed himself instead. His death was the ultimate sacrifice; the one that reconciled everyone to God. The old ways – animal sacrifices and circumcision – could never save us; only faith in Jesus could do that.

Acts 15.3–35

After a lot of debate, Peter took Paul's side, arguing that both Jew and Gentile would be saved by faith. But the man who really swings it is the church leader, James the brother of Jesus. A righteous, disciplined, God-fearing Jew, he was respected by all sides.[2] Now this devout Jew chooses the least comfortable path. In the issue of whether Christians should be circumcised, he ticks the 'No' box. It is about faith. He knew he was going to get grief from the Judaizers in Jerusalem.

Acts 15.36–41

But he also knew the gospel was greater than they had previously understood, great enough to encompass everybody.

1 There were other issues as well. Judaism was a *religio licta* (i.e. a legally recognised religion). But Christianity? How would the Romans view that?

2 Hence his nickname; 'James the Just.'

5.5 Paul's Journeys

So Paul starts a series of journeys, crossing many years and covering many miles, through Asia and across into Greece. Acts 16.1–10

He picks up followers on the way: Timothy from Lystra, Luke, the doctor from Philippi and Lydia, a business-woman who is the first convert on European soil. Acts 16.1–3, 11–15

His words cause ripples. He is jailed in Philippi and rescued through a miraculous earthquake. He inspires riots in Thessalonica and Ephesus. He baffles the philosophers in Athens. In Corinth the Jews haul Paul before the proconsul Gallio. He dismisses the charges as a mere religious dispute, paving the way for Christianity to spread throughout the Roman empire. Acts 16.16–17.9, 19.1–41 Acts 17.16–34, 18.12–17

Paul supports himself by his trade as a tentmaker. He establishes churches, heals rifts, challenges false teaching, and writes letters filled with practical advice, heartfelt discipline and wonderful, wonderful words of love. Acts 18.1–4

There are miracles; healings and earthquakes and angelic appearances. (At Troas a boy is restored to life after dropping off during Paul's talk and falling out of a third-storey window.) Acts 20.7–12

Finally he returns to Jerusalem where he is arrested (on trumped-up charges) and spends two years in jail in Caesarea. After preaching to the governor and the King, he is sent to Rome for trial. After a horrendous journey, when they are shipwrecked on Malta, he arrives in Italy. Acts 21.1–23.35 Acts 27.1–28.16

And my 84th point is...

I'm trying to remain philosophical about this.

In Rome, under house arrest, Paul continues to spread the word, writing and talking about the great Rescuer, Jesus, to anyone who will listen.

Acts 28.16–31

In later years, Paul's letters are collected and writers start to compile accounts of Jesus' life and teaching. John Mark's account is based on the recollections of Peter; Luke – in Rome with Paul – records a two-part history (a life of Jesus and an account of the young church) for a Roman official; Matthew writes his account for Jews. (While John waits and thinks and ponders and prays.)

Lk 1.1–4; Acts 1.1–2

Col 3.8–11

The new church crosses boundaries – geographical, political and social. Followers include slaves and free, Jew, Gentile, Greeks, Romans. No boundaries any more. No limits.

Throughout, Paul follows his Master's example. Like Jesus, he goes to Jerusalem, though he knows it will mean arrest and even death. (And, like so many other characters in the Big Story, his journey leads him to a new understanding of who he is and who God is.)

He ends in Rome, the centre of the empire, the hub of the wheel. And there, according to tradition, he dies.[1] His letters become the first Scriptures of the Christian church.[2] As years pass and the original witnesses die, accounts of Jesus' life are drawn together from eye-witness recollections and collections of the Master's sayings. Four of these gospels – each with their own unique flavour – are accepted by the early Church as reliable accounts.

1 Probably in the mid-60s AD. Beheaded during persecution unleashed by Nero.

2 The letters date from the mid-50s AD onwards.

5.6 The Fall of the Temple

Eventually the Romans clamp down on the church. Many Christians are arrested and killed. Peter writes to encourage Christians under pressure, but, like his master, he is crucified in Rome.

Back in Jerusalem the tension increases. James, the brother of Christ, is stoned to death. In response to a warning from God, the Christians in Jerusalem leave the city and settle in a place called Pella, across the Jordan.

Then it all kicks off. The Jews rebel against the Romans. It starts when Florus, the Roman procurator, takes silver from the temple. The Roman garrison in Jerusalem is attacked. Reinforcements arrive, but the insurgents defeat them as well.

Rome does not tolerate loss. Sixty thousand heavily armed troops roll into Palestine, slaughtering thousands and crushing Jerusalem in an orgy of destruction. The magnificent temple is destroyed and its treasures taken to Rome.

Utter, utter ruin. The temple is wrecked, the city is destroyed. The prophecies of Jesus have all come true. It feels like the end.

1 Pet 1.1–9

Mt 24.1–2; Mk 13.1–2; Lk 21.5–24

The end of the temple brings to a close one of the key story-lines of the Old Testament.

During his years on earth, Jesus predicted the fall of the temple, and in 70AD his prediction came true. The Romans crush the Jewish rebellion; the temple is burned to the ground and its treasures carted off to Rome. One thousand years of history gone. Early church tradition relates how the Christians were warned by 'a revelation' to evacuate the city, thus escaping the destruction, caused by the Roman army.[1]

Elsewhere they could not escape. In 64AD, there is a disastrous fire in Rome. The Emperor Nero looks around for someone to blame and chooses the Christians. In the months that follow, many Christians are killed in the most horrific ways, including, probably Peter and Paul.[2]

The fate of most of the apostles is unknown. The Bible tells us of the death of James, brother of John. It hints about the death of Peter. But for the rest, there is little, just scraps of tradition.[3] What we do know is that thousands of followers die for their faith.

Yet the persecution only strengthens the cause. When non-Christians see how these Christians die, many start to wonder...

---

1 Eusebius, *History of the Church* 3.5.3. Go on, admit it. Secretly you're impressed.

2 Tacitus records that 'in their deaths they were made the subjects of sport; for they were wrapped in the hides of wild beasts and torn to pieces by dogs, or nailed to crosses, or set on fire, and when day declined, were burned to serve for nocturnal lights.' Tacitus, *Annals* 15.44

3 Early tradition suggests Philip died in Hierapolis in Asia Minor and Andrew was crucified on an 'X' shaped cross. Despite the fact that this cross later became the flag of Scotland, it is more likely that he died in Scythia than in Glasgow.

5.7 New Heaven, New Earth

Back to John. Old, but fighting. He writes to churches to fight false teaching, spread by itinerant teachers. He writes his gospel, a deep, dazzling account of Jesus' life and teaching.

Suddenly a new wave of persecution breaks out against the church. And John, old as he is, is sent to a prison-island called Patmos. There he sees a vision of the end. It has many things, this vision. A jumble of pictures and images from throughout the years. Great beasts and terrifying horsemen, angels and lambs and trumpets and great, shattering battles raging over the earth.

Most of all, he sees how it is all going to end.

The tale that began with the creation of the heavens and the earth, will end in a new heaven and a new earth. God, the Author of the tale, will put all things right, bring it round, full circle. God will live with men. No barriers, just as it was in the be ginning. Only better.

That's how it ends, the Big Story.

All this John sees, staring out over the sea from his rocky prison. Not defeat, but victory. Not destruction by some petty Roman emperor but eternal glory for the King of Kings.

Not the end, but a new beginning.

A whole new story, bigger and brighter and more beautiful than before.

Talk about a happy ending.

OK, first one to reach the pub gets a round in.

John spent much of the latter part of his life combatting false teachers, called gnostics. Gnosticism was all about secrecy.[1] It was religious snobbery, holding that there were some truths which were too special for ordinary, common believers.

That's not Christ's way, argues John. Christ came to show us God. Christ says, 'Here's the truth now come on in.' Nothing is hidden, or kept back for a 'special' group of people. The curtain has been torn down. Access all areas.

Rev 1.9–11

Rev 5.1–14, 6.1–8, 11.15–12.18, 19.1–21

Then, on a small island, a tiny wilderness, John sees a huge vision. Revelation, the book which records what he saw, is not only a picture of what will happen at the end of time,[2] it's a picture of what has *already* happened. Christ appears in the vision as 'the lamb', whose death has 'bought for God people from every tribe, language, nation, and race.' Victory is not in doubt; John is imprisoned, but he knows he is on the winning side. 'I've seen the future,' writes John. 'God wins.'

Rev 21.1–22.21

That's the end of the Big Story. God wins. Humans and God will live together for eternity. Nothing hidden, no secrecy.

That's what John sees. Christ has saved us.

And God wins.

2 Jn 7

1 Gnosticism comes from the Greek word *gnosis*, meaning 'hidden knowledge'. So gnostics were revealing 'hidden' truths, (e.g. Christ wasn't really human, but some kind of spirit. Or the world wasn't made by God but by some lesser being.) They backed these up by writing spurious 'gospels'. The church rejected these not because they contained hidden truths, but because (a) they were written between 150 and 200 years after Christ, and (b) they were silly. (And the idea that Jesus was married to Mary Magdalene and emigrated to France, was not a gnostic belief. Even the gnostics weren't that stupid. Even heretics have standards.)

2 A picture, not a timetable. Beware anyone who claims to know when things it describes are going to happen. Only God knows that.

Once after time has finished there is a Great Big God...

The Big Story: Key Themes

Here are just some of the key themes that we've spotted as we've travelled through the Big Story. There are more, but that's the thing about the Big Story: there is always more.

The Miraculous Rescue

God is always rescuing his people. We see the Israelites rescued from Egypt, from various warring nations and from Assyria. We see individuals rescued from perilous situations (e.g. Daniel in the lions' den). Sometimes this rescue is couched in terms of redemption – the buying back of someone from slavery. And most of all, we see the ultimate rescue – from death itself.

The Wilderness Encounter

Individuals and nations go off into a wilderness, where God makes himself known to them. Sometimes he is actually visible; often he meets people through visions or by encouraging them, challenging them or refreshing them for their journey. Frequently these meetings are associated with mountains or deserts.

The Younger Son

God's chooses whom he will bless. We see this with Jacob, but also in events like the blessing of Joseph's youngest son and the choice of David (the eighth son of Jesse). Later, Jesus 'broadens' this theme: choosing for his followers people who would normally be left out, showing how God's choice extends to other people, other nations.

The Enduring Promise

At key points in the Big Story, God makes a promise. This agreement, or covenant, is the basis for the relationship between God and his people. He makes promises to Abraham, to Noah and to David. Jesus, in the last supper, ushers in a new covenant, a new promise based not on obeying the law, but on accepting his forgiveness.

The Right Way

Throughout the Big Story there is an emphasis on obedience. Bad things happen when people do not obey God. Children die, kingdoms are lost, nations are destroyed. Often we see disobedience occurs when people have been rescued or reached their goal. At that point, they relax, let down their guard (e.g. the Israelites in the wilderness, David on the throne, the entire Judges period).

The New Name

Names matter. People are given new names, people change their names. Names express ownership, purpose, commitment. God renames Abraham, Jesus renames Peter.

The God who Lingers

God has no need to explain himself and is under no obligation to tell humans what he plans. But he does anyway. Why? Because he is friends with them. Because they are his children. Throughout the Big Story we see God exceed expectations.

The Unexpected Child

Most frequently born to elderly parents, these children are born for a purpose and to play a particular, unique role in the Big Story. From Abraham and Sarah, to Zechariah and Elizabeth, we see parents who have given up hope granted the blessing of children.

The Perfect Sacrifice

Sacrifices loom large in this story. People offer sacrifices to give thanks (e.g. Noah), to show obedience and faith in God (e.g. Abraham) or to say 'sorry' for sins (e.g. Israel – frequently). This theme reaches its pinnacle in Christ, who is seen as the one, complete sacrifice, restoring the relationship between God and humanity.

The Return to Life

The biggie. The deepest, most fundamental theme. There are real rebirths – dead people brought back to life. There are symbolic rebirths, where people lose everything and God remakes, and often renames them. Sometimes these are accompanied by physical journeys (e.g. Jonah in the fish); sometimes by symbolic actions (e.g. baptism in the River Jordan). It's certainly a spiritual 'rebirth'; Jesus said to one follower that it was impossible to enter the kingdom of God without making this fresh, new start.

Many, if not all, of the themes listed above are part of this one. So, we see captives, barren mothers, outcast 'younger sons'; and suddenly they are saved, pregnant, chosen. People walk into the dead wilderness and come out glowing. People are renamed, restarted for a new life and a new purpose. Death and rebirth. God bringing back people, nations, the entire world from the dead.

This is the story beneath the Big Story. Death is not final. With God, there is always rebirth.

If you want.

The Big Story and You

The Big Story isn't ended. It rolls on, and will do so, until the final days that John saw from his island prison.

In the meantime, we all have a role to play, and we can all respond to the themes.

So, one last thing to think about. Those themes – the ten themes listed on the previous page. Have you seen them in your life?

For example, you might feel like you're in the wilderness just now. If so, we can take heart from the Big Story because, hard as the wilderness is, it is a place where people meet God.

Or perhaps you're comfortable, perhaps everything in the garden is rosy. Great. But the Big Story shows us that those are the times when we have to be on our guard. Obedience to God is vital.

Or maybe, you've never really experienced the new birth that the followers of Jesus all experience. Maybe you're waiting, holding back. Maybe you just need to say sorry to him and ask him to help you start again.

All I'm saying is that we are all in the Big Story, right here, right now. It swirls around us, it forms, whether we know it or not, the backdrop to our lives.

It is such a Big Story, you see, that there is room for all of us.